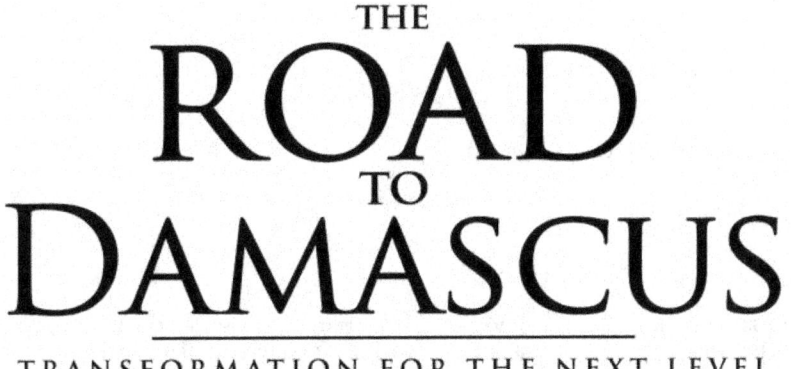

THE ROAD TO DAMASCUS

TRANSFORMATION FOR THE NEXT LEVEL

SECOND EDITION

By
MARKITA BROOKS

THE ROAD TO DAMASCUS
TRANSFORMATION FOR THE NEXT LEVEL

By Markita Brooks

Copyright © 2019   Markita Brooks

Second Edition

ISBN 978-1-7322243-2-2

Christian Living: Calling & Vocation • Christian Living: Personal Growth • Christian Ministry: General • Religion : Messianic Judaism

Cover design and layout by Kennesha M. Walker of Miwa Design and Graphics www.designmiwa.com

Printed in the United States of America

Scripture quotations are taken from the Complete Jewish Bible, copyright © 1998 by David H. Stern. Published by Jewish New Testament Publications, Inc., P.O. Box 615, Clarksville, Maryland 21029. www.messianicjewish.net/jntp. Used by permission.

Scripture quotations marked (NIV) are taken from the HOLY BIBLE, NEW INTERNATIONAL VERSION®. NIV®. Copyright© 1973, 1978, 1984 by International Bible Society. Used by permission of Zondervan. All rights reserved.

The Eleventh Step is reprinted with permission of Alcoholics Anonymous World Services, Inc. (AAWS) Permission to reprint the Eleventh Step does not mean that AAWS has reviewed or approved the contents of this publication, or that AAWS necessarily agrees with the views expressed herein. A.A. is a program of recovery from alcoholism only - use of the Eleventh Step in connection with programs and activities which are patterned after A.A., but which address other problems, or in any other non-A.A. context, does not imply otherwise.   Additionally, while A.A. is a spiritual program, A.A. is not a religious program. Thus, A.A. is not affiliated or allied with any sect, denomination, or specific religious belief.

DEDICATION

This book is dedicated to:

God (Father, Son and Holy Spirit)
and the work of ministry to which He has called me

and to

My children who have your own personal experiences with the Messiah. I pray that they are even more exciting and intimate than mine have been.

THANK YOU

I thank God for:

The love, guidance and support of my family, especially my husband, mother and father

and for

Rabbi Eric Carlson and Apostle Allison Smith (God rest her soul) who have allowed God to use them to train me, so that I might be a useful vessel in the eyes of my Creator.

TABLE OF CONTENTS

A Letter From the Author..1
Introduction..4
    Chapter 1: The Need for Transformation.......................5

Part I: Saved from Death..18
    Chapter 2: On a Road to Destruction............................19
    Chapter 3: Detoured by Yeshua....................................34
    Chapter 4: Making a U-Turn...41
    Chapter 5: Walking With Adonai:
        "Markita's Testimony"...................................52

Part II: Transformed into the Messiah's Image..........58
    Chapter 6: Immersed..59
    Chapter 7: Born Again..84
    Chapter 8: Saved, Sanctified and Holy Ghost Filled:
        "Regina's Testimony"....................................98

Part III: Used by God..102
    Chapter 9: Sharing the Good News.............................103
    Chapter 10: Serving the Body.......................................120
    Chapter 11: Putting Feet on My Faith:
        "James' Testimony".....................................148

Conclusion..152
    Chapter 12: Extended Transforming Experiences......153

Endnotes..172

A LETTER FROM THE AUTHOR

Beloved,

I praise God that He ordained for you to walk with me on the Road to Damascus. It has been an exciting and powerful journey for me so far, as He continues to transform me while using me to deliver an invitation to be transformed to all those who are part of the Body of the Messiah. Because we are in the end times and the Messiah is soon to return, God is restoring order and authority to the Body of Believers by raising up the Messianic community. The Messianic community supersedes the "Church", as it consists of all believers, both Jews and Gentiles, as more than just worshippers, but children of God and citizens of His Kingdom.

To bring order to His House and walk in the full authority of the Messiah, we must return to our roots, which are the Jewish faith and culture, and our source, which is the Word of God. To line up this book with God's will to transform the Body, the Son of God will be referred to as Yeshua the Messiah (Jesus Christ), His Name in the original Hebrew, and all followers of the Messiah will be called "believers". Children of Isra'el and places in Isra'el will be referred to by their original names in Hebrew as well (with a parenthetical translation), but books of the Bible, even those named after people, will remain in their English translation for easy referencing. Locations outside of Isra'el will also remain in their English translation.

All of the Scripture texts used in this book come from the *Complete Jewish Bible*, translated by David H. Stern, unless otherwise noted. Though this version of the Bible is translated into English, God used its translator to clearly represent Jewish faith and culture in the translation. This is important for us as we come together in the Body, because most of us do not speak Hebrew (or Greek) and miss important revelations that are lost in translation. Because Yeshua and the early leaders of the Body are all children of Isra'el, receiving a clear understanding of the Jewish faith and culture are essential to all believers for they are the faith and culture established by God and used by Him to redeem the world. As God prepares us to worship Him together, we must accept the invitation to study His Word together. For this reason, I have included lots of Scripture quotes and endnotes in this book, for it is the Word of God that transforms. You may follow along with whatever version of the Bible that's comfortable for you. Just be sure to read the Scriptures for yourself, as the Bible is the infallible Word of God, the Source of our knowledge and wisdom; for it, there is no substitute.

I am confident that Adonai (the Lord) is using more than just this book to speak to you at this point in your life. In Yeshua's (Jesus') Name, I pray that you will have eyes to see, ears to hear, a heart to understand and turn so that the Messiah may heal you. Now, let us pray together as we allow God to draw us closer to Himself and thus closer to each other:

> "ADONAI Elohim (LORD God), Creator of all things, Ruler of the universe, we worship you for your awesome power and might. We bless you for your goodness and mercy towards us, which is new every day. Father, we realize that as individual believers and a collective Body we often misunderstand and disobey your will, so we humbly ask that you reveal yourself to us in a new way. Help us to hear you and see you in the events of our day. Teach us more about your holiness so that we might know enough to acknowledge our sin before you. Expose every secret sin area in our lives, and reveal every hidden motive in our hearts. We are incapable of cleansing ourselves and serving your people, so take control at this very moment. Open our eyes to see as you see, open our hearts to feel as you feel and shower us with your unfailing love. Let us not take you for granted. Teach us to love each other as you love us. Remove all judgment, prejudice and bitterness in our hearts. Begin a transformation within us right now, so that each day we will come closer to the image of your Son and come together to represent you to the world. Make our lives living testimonies to the world, and use us in the lives and transformations of others. In your good pleasure, bring shalom (peace, rest, wholeness) to

Isra'el as well. Cover your Holy Land with your grace and protect her from all enemies. Expand her borders and rebuke every person who seeks to diminish or destroy her. Make her a praise in all the earth. Do this all for your glory and for our good. In the Name of Yeshua (Jesus) we pray. Amen."

Be blessed in Adonai (the Lord) today and always.

Your sister in the Messiah,
Markita Brooks

INTRODUCTION
THE NEED FOR TRANSFORMATION

"In other words, do not let yourselves be conformed to the standards of the 'olam hazeh [this world]. Instead, keep letting yourselves be transformed by the renewing of your minds; so that you will know what God wants and will agree that it is good, satisfying and able to succeed."

Romans 12:2

CHAPTER 1
THE NEED FOR TRANSFORMATION

"For God so loved the world that he gave his only and unique Son, so that everyone who trusts in him may have eternal life, instead of being utterly destroyed."
— John 3:16

"Just to be close to You. Just to be close to You. Just to be close to You . . . is my desire." Adonai (the Lord) used this sweet little hymn to awaken me this morning. I get a song every morning in my spirit, a song that speaks directly to me. I don't use an alarm clock anymore. I simply wait for my spiritual clock radio to wake me. It prepares me for my morning quiet time with Him, which prepares my spirit, heart and mind for whatever I'll encounter during the day. In my time with God this morning, He reminded me not to forsake the intimacy He and I share in our relationship. As a wife, mother, business owner and ministry leader, it's hard not to get bogged down with tasks and meeting the needs of those around me. But my first love just wanted some quality time alone with me today. It's nice to be desired by God.

God adores me, and I have no doubts about that. Not because I'm righteous, or because I work hard for Him, but because I am His and He is mine.[1] He loves you in this same way. My prayer for you is that you would receive God's passionate love and allow it to flow into every area of your life; that's transformation.

God loves us, you and me, so much that He sent His Son as a sacrifice to destroy every barrier between us and the perfect and wise Father. It is Yeshua (Jesus) who extends the invitation to receive the precious gift of salvation from the consequences of our sins, which is death.[2] Our loving and merciful Father takes it a step further though. After we've accepted His salvation from eternal death, God keeps sending Yeshua (Jesus) to us to save us from death on earth, in every form,[3] and prepare us for eternal fellowship. In short, He sends His Son over and over again to draw us closer to Himself. The

Messiah comes, and keeps coming, to continually transform us into His image,[4] making us sons of El 'Elyon (God Most High) who are prepared to receive our eternal inheritance of life forever in His presence.[5]

Each of us has a piece of God in him. However, Yeshua the Messiah (Jesus Christ) is the only human in creation who contains all of the characteristics of God in their fullness,[6] being fully man AND fully God. It is He whom God sent down to earth to bear the sins of mankind, and it is He whom God continues to send to empower us to exist in the fullness of God as well.[7]

The Scripture text from Romans 12:2 on the "Introduction" page is taken from the <u>Complete Jewish Bible</u>. You will note that this particular translation reads, "keep letting yourselves be transformed," rather than, "be ye transformed." As I spend time reading Scripture from a Jewish cultural perspective, I understand that most of the processes mentioned in the Bible are ongoing cycles, spiraling upward when guided by God and spiraling downward apart from God. Unlike Scripture written from a Western cultural mindset, the only final destination is death. Until death, from the Jewish perspective, we never arrive at any place or achieve anything in this life, but rather we continue to learn and grow and change. That's what this book is about, the continual transformation of God's people into the image of the Messiah, so that the Body of Believers (a.k.a. the Bride) will continually be prepared for union with her Bridegroom.[8]

As children of El 'Elyon (God Most High), we are in danger of spiritual stagnation leading to spiritual death whenever we stop allowing God to transform us. When we become comfortable in our relationship with Him or our position in the Kingdom, we close our ears to His voice that always speaks new life for new levels. Each time He desires to elevate us and draw us closer to Himself, we need yet another transformation so that we will "know what God wants and will agree that it is good, satisfying and able to succeed."

Going to the next level sounds wonderful, but our comfort with the current level will always compete for our loyalty. Every time God wants to draw us closer to Himself and elevate us in His Kingdom, we must sacrifice the comfort we now feel because we've mastered some things and achieved some success on this level. Moving on to the next level for many of us is like starting over. And in many ways, we are starting over. Remember it is a spiral, either going up or down, so the process will be repeated. Each time, it should be on a higher plane though. This is why we must keep letting ourselves be transformed. Otherwise, we will not agree with God that going to the next level is good, satisfying and able to succeed.

Each level is more challenging as it brings greater glory to God and requires greater sacrifice from us. Yet the things we learned and the strength we received on the previous levels prepare us for the next. Moving to the next level for Yochanan the Immerser (John the Baptist) meant leaving a thriving ministry in the desert to await execution in prison. He was prepared for that level by the self-sacrificing lifestyle he led.[9] Then immersing Yeshua (Jesus) in the Yarden (Jordan) River[10] provided the transformation he needed to understand and agree with God's will for his next level move.[11] Are you ready for the next level?

The Invitation

The Messiah comes to us when God knows that He's prepared us to be transformed in an area of our lives. The Father sends His Son when we're at low points, crying out to Him. It's only at these low points that we can truly allow deliverance to transform us—deliverance from our present status or situation—because we're ready to give up the comfort of our current level for something more. It's then that Yeshua (Jesus) reveals Himself to us as our personal Deliverer, for the first or fiftieth time.

Yeshua (Jesus) said that He came for sinners, not the righteous,[12] the sick, not the healthy[13]. In these phrases, He tells us that we must first recognize that we are sin-sick sinners to accept His deliverance. We shut Yeshua out of every area of our lives that we feel we can handle on our own. That type of independence and self-righteousness will always hinder us from being transformed by our Deliverer. Here's a good example. There was a woman who washed Yeshua's feet with her tears and dried them with her hair, just before pouring perfume on His feet. The Messiah contrasted her with the religious leader named Shim'on (Simon) who witnessed this act and judged the woman as a sinner. Yeshua answered him with a story.

"'A certain creditor had two debtors; the one owed ten times as much as the other. When they were unable to pay him back, he canceled both their debts. Now which of them will love him more?' Shim'on answered, 'I suppose the one for whom he canceled the larger debt.' 'Your judgment is right,' Yeshua said to him.

"Then turning to the woman, he said to Shim'on, 'Do you see this woman? I came into your house—you didn't give me water for my feet, but this woman has washed my feet with her tears and dried them with her hair! You didn't give me a kiss; but from the time I arrived, this woman has not stopped kissing my feet! You didn't put oil on my head, but this woman poured perfume on my feet! Because of this, I tell you that her sins—which are many!—have been forgiven, because she loved much. But someone who has been forgiven only a little loves only a little.' Then he said to her, 'Your sins have been forgiven.'"[14]

In this story, Yeshua points out that the religious leader was also a sinner, though his sins were not as blatant as the woman's. Like the religious leader, we won't accept the Messiah's deliverance if we don't think we need forgiveness. That's why God often sends His Son when we're at those low points. This keeps us from being self-righteous like the religious leader and failing to appreciate the gift of deliverance. Yeshua forgives sins, the subtle and hidden as well as the obvious and blatant. In order to go to another level in Him, we must allow Him to show us the sin currently in us that can't go with us to the next level. Usually, these are things that seem insignificant to us on this level, and we may not even consider them sins. He knows us though, and desires to prepare us and transform us to meet the challenges He's positioning us to face.

We all sin and fall short of the glory of God.[15] First John 1:8 reads, "If we claim not to have sin, we are deceiving ourselves, and the truth is not in us." Our sin separates us from a holy, sinless God. Therefore, every attempt on His part to draw us closer to Himself and transform us more into the image of the Messiah will include deliverance from sin. The key to deliverance is openly acknowledging that we are sinners (confession), submitting ourselves to God (submission), and accepting His forgiveness through the Messiah (acceptance), which empowers us to turn away from our sins (repentance).

Transformation of Jews and Christians

This process of confession, submission, acceptance and repentance must continue throughout our lives as believers. When we accept Yeshua the Messiah (Jesus Christ) as our Deliverer, we receive forgiveness for the sins we've committed, but we still have to deal with the sins we will commit and how to stop committing them. In the Torah (Law of Moses), the children of Isra'el presented sin offerings to God more than once in their lifetimes. Sacrifices had to be made continually in order to receive atonement and cleansing of sins. Yeshua made the ultimate sacrifice once and for all. However, we must present ourselves to Him on an on-going basis to apply His blood to the newly uncovered areas of sin in our lives. Without blood, there is no atonement of sins.[16] In this way, we continually receive atonement and cleansing of our sins until we become the people He died for us to be. He desires that we would truly be set free from slavery to sin in our hearts, not just forgiven of our acts. This freedom comes only from an ever-intensifying intimate relationship with Him, as He empowers us to be holy in the presence of a Holy God.

As God's children, whether Jew or Christian, we often assume that our position in the Father's Kingdom is secure. However, there is always something we must do to meet God where He's working. We must be committed to allowing Yeshua to transform us into representations of Himself. The emissary Sha'ul (apostle Paul) said that we must work out our salvation with fear and trembling.[17] This acknowledges our need for a Deliverer and the requirement for us to surrender ourselves to Him daily, that we might be changed. The transformation from sinner to servant is not an easy one, and it takes all of our lives to complete. We can't do it in our own strength, and we can't restrict Him to doing it in our lives only part-time.

Our deliverance requires more than just believing that Yeshua is who He says He is. We must acknowledge with our mouths that He is Adonai (Lord and Master): Adonai over our lives, our decisions and our actions. By claiming Him as Adonai, we surrender to Him power and authority over ourselves and everything we own, so that He might lead us. Ya'akov (James), the brother of Yeshua and leader of the body of believers in Yerushalayim (Jerusalem), admonished believers for not living the words they believed and lining up their actions with their faith. He said, "But someone will say that you have faith and I have actions. Show me this faith of yours without the actions, and I will show you my faith by my actions! You believe that 'God is one'? Good for you! The demons believe it too—the thought makes them shudder with fear!"[18]

We can believe that Yeshua died for our sins without surrendering ourselves to Him completely. "If it seems bad to you to serve ADONAI (the LORD), then choose today whom you are going to serve! Will it be the gods your ancestors served beyond the River? or the gods of the Emori, in whose land you are living? As for me and my household, we will serve ADONAI!"[19] We will be slaves to our flesh, which is sinful, or slaves to the Messiah; there are no other options and no middle ground.[20] A slave does not make her own decisions; instead she does everything her master commands her to do. This is what our LORD requires of us, and He will settle for nothing less.

Transformation of the Body of the Messiah

Because Yeshua is close to returning, He is currently taking the global Body of the Messiah through a transforming experience just as its members are all being transformed. The House of God is being set in order that we might take our rightful place in the physical and spiritual realms. We've not been able to do so in the full power of the Messiah because of the disorder and lack of authority in the Body. The disorder is caused by the absence of the children of Isra'el from the Body of the Messiah, which we will now explore. The lack of authority comes from not fulfilling all five of the five-fold commissions,[21] which we will explore in chapter 10. In these last days, Yeshua has been working overtime to restore both order and authority to His Body, though. We must meet Him where He is working.

In the last few decades, the children of Isra'el have begun to openly acknowledge Yeshua as the Messiah in large numbers. Rather than "converting" to Christianity, which would strip you of your heritage and rob Christians of the wealth of knowledge and history you've preserved as a people, God has instead begun to teach the children of Isra'el how to receive the Jewish Messiah as Jews. This empowers Messianic Jews to train Christians through the strengths and wisdom He has developed in His people Isra'el over the millennia, placing you in a unique position in the Body of the Messiah that, since the early formation of the Body of Believers, has been left unfilled. It also releases Gentile believers to worship God freely in accordance with your varying cultures and heritages, rather than feeling that you must worship in accordance with the culture and heritage of the people group who first presented the Good News to your people. In years to come, believers will gain new insight and understanding of the will of God through this and other transforming experiences in the Body. This new understanding, when coupled with obedience, will position us for greater blessings from Adonai, which will increase our power to change the world.

It was always God's intention that Isra'el and the nations would come together in worship of Him. It's a part of

God's promise to Avraham (Abraham) in Genesis 12:3 and 22:18, to Yitz'chak (Isaac) in Genesis 26:4, and it was prophesied in Isaiah 49:6. The emissary Sha'ul (apostle Paul) addresses the union of Gentiles, who were far off, and the children of Isra'el, who were nearby, in Ephesians 2:11-22, in which he states the following:

> "But now, you who were once far off have been brought near through the shedding of the Messiah's blood. For he himself is our shalom (peace, wholeness)—he has made us both one and has broken down the m'chitzah (dividing wall) which divided us by destroying in his own body the enmity occasioned by the Torah (Law of Moses), with its commands set forth in the form of ordinances. He did this in order to create in union with himself from the two groups a single new humanity and thus make shalom, and in order to reconcile to God both in a single body by being executed on a stake as a criminal and thus in himself killing that enmity. Also, when he came, he announced as Good News shalom to you far off and shalom to those nearby, news that through him we both have access in one Spirit to the Father. So then, you are no longer foreigners and strangers. On the contrary, you are fellow citizens with God's people and members of God's family. You have been built on the foundation of the emissaries and prophets, with the cornerstone being Yeshua the Messiah himself. In union with him the whole building is held together, and it is growing into a holy temple in union with the Lord. Yes, in union with him; you yourselves are being built together into a spiritual dwelling-place for God!"

Until recently, the children of Isra'el have been delayed in accepting Yeshua as the Messiah, however. In Romans 11:25-26 Sha'ul (Paul) states,

> "For, brothers, I want you to understand the truth which God formerly concealed but has now revealed, so that

you won't imagine you know more than you actually do. It is that stoniness, to a degree, has come upon Isra'el, until the Gentile world enters in its fullness; and that it is in this way that all Isra'el will be saved. As the Tanakh (Old Testament) says, 'Out of Tziyon (Zion) will come the Redeemer; he will turn away ungodliness from Ya'akov (Jacob) and this will be my covenant with them, . . . when I take away their sins.'"

The Scriptures above confirm that the acceptance of Yeshua as the Messiah by the children of Isra'el is an essential transforming experience for the Body of the Messiah.[22]

Throughout our study on transformation, we will look at the most well-known example: the first transforming experience of Sha'ul (Paul), the emissary (apostle) God used to write the Scriptures above. The emissary Sha'ul was a devout Jew and Parush (Pharisee),[23] yet the Messiah transformed him into an emissary (apostle) to the Gentiles. His ministry to Gentiles was instrumental in the early formation of the Body of Believers throughout the world. Despite his dedication to his mission to Gentiles, Sha'ul never forgot his brothers; in fact, his love for Isra'el and desire that all Isra'el be saved continued to grow.[24] He is an excellent example for us to study because of his deep love for both Jews and Gentiles. Hence, he shares the Word of God without bias or taint and always with the goal of uniting the Body of Believers. His many transforming experiences helped to make that possible.

Because he's not one of the original twelve emissaries and is stopped by Yeshua while on his way to persecute believers, Sha'ul maintains a humble devotion to God throughout his ministry. He's not arrogant with Jews or Gentiles and welcomes all into the Kingdom. His testimony is an example for us of the power of transformation in the life of a believer and in the Body of the Messiah. If God can use Sha'ul to set the world on fire for Yeshua, surely He can use you and me.

A Young Man Named Sha'ul

At the beginning of Acts chapter 9, we become acquainted with Sha'ul (Paul), a young Parush (Pharisee). Our brief introduction to him in Acts chapter 8, verses 1 and 3, reveals that he approved of the stoning of Stephen, a believer full of God's grace and power,[25] and that he began to destroy the community of believers by going from house to house dragging off men and women and putting them in prison. Chapter 9, however, begins to really depict his zeal for persecuting believers. Not only did he carry out assignments from the chief priests, but he also requested an opportunity to pursue believers outside of Y'hudah (Judea) and bring them back to Yerushalayim (Jerusalem) for persecution. It was on his mission to Damascus that Sha'ul encountered Yeshua and was changed forever.

Beloved, we can have transforming experiences like that of Sha'ul, provided we answer Yeshua's calls when He comes to us. Before the Messiah reveals our folly to us, we make decisions for ourselves based on our flawed thinking.[26] Proverbs 14:12 reads, "There can be a way that seems right to a person, but at its end are the ways of death." This Scripture is not just referring to eternal death away from the Father, but also to death in areas of our lives and souls. This Scripture is proved true in our Biblical example of Sha'ul. He actually believed he was fervently serving God by persecuting those who belonged to "the Way."[27] He used his formal education about the Torah (Law), his religious training in "justice" and his recollection of the story of Akhan's (Achan's) stoning[28] to justify his sinful thirst for blood. Sha'ul was a violent man,[29] and the wrath in him found a legal and socially acceptable way to live out its desires. Such thinking will always lead us down a road to destruction. Though Sha'ul thought the road to Damascus was leading to the deaths of believers in the Messiah, it was in fact leading to his own spiritual death.

We all desire certain things in our flesh; we're all inclined to particular sins. And much like, Sha'ul, we all continue to carry religious ideals created by people, from both Christianity and Judaism, that are not Scripturally sound and stand in opposition to the true heart of God for unity within the Body of Believers. Without the help of Yeshua, we'll continue to structure our lives around feeding those desires and religious ideals, long after we've accepted Him as Adonai (Lord) and Deliverer. The people with whom we associate, the ways in which we worship, the jobs we choose, the clothes we wear, how we plan our days and many other decisions are often predicated on whether or not they will help us fulfill our desires and uphold the ideals within us. Feeding our desires and upholding our ideals is comfortable; it creates the least amount of conflict with others and within ourselves, that is, until Yeshua shows up.

Sha'ul believed that he was on a road to success, to rewards from man and God, and to self-fulfillment. We can't see that destruction lies ahead unless Yeshua points it out to us. We've been trained our entire lives, even among God's people, to see only what we want to see, just as Sha'ul was. It's not until God uses the Light of the World[30] to grab our attention that we have the opportunity to see and accept the truth: we are STILL sinners and our sins lead us to death.[31] The Messiah is the detour sign on our road to Damascus, a.k.a. destruction. He came that we may have life in its fullest measure,[32] and every area of our souls that is undelivered is an area of death in us. Who among us would continue to drive down a road with signs marked "Danger Ahead: Steep Cliff"? No one in their right mind would do that, but we often continue on those roads, in the spiritual sense, in various areas of our lives. We do this because we're NOT in our right minds.

In Romans 8:1-14, the emissary Sha'ul (apostle Paul) addresses the sinful nature and the mind controlled by it. Such a mind is unable to submit to God.[33] Romans 12:1-2 explains the transformation process from living according to the sinful nature to living in accordance with the Spirit of God. Simply put, it consists of sacrificing our bodies, not conforming to the world (which includes man-made religious systems), and renewing our minds to know (and live out) the perfect will of God. God was able to use Sha'ul to deliver this message of transformation because of his personal transforming experiences. He himself was transformed from a sinful, religious man headed toward death into a son of El 'Elyon (God Most High), not only guaranteed life in its fullest measure but also leading others to it as well.

As we journey through this book together, allow the Ruach HaKodesh (Holy Spirit) to reveal to you the divine perfection of Sha'ul's first transforming experience, depicted in Acts 9:1-22, and explore similar testimonies of transformation from myself and others. God still speaks. God still redeems. God still saves souls. To live with Him forever, we must allow His Son to transform us from sinners to servants. Times change, people change, but God does not change.[34] His will for us is the same as it was when He sent His Son to die for our sins: He wishes that none would be lost.[35]

PART I
SAVED FROM DEATH

"That if you acknowledge publicly with your mouth that Yeshua is Lord and trust in your heart that God raised him from the dead, you will be delivered."

Romans 10:9

CHAPTER 2
ON A ROAD TO DESTRUCTION

"Go in through the narrow gate; for the gate that leads to destruction is wide and the road broad, and many travel it; but it is a narrow gate and a hard road that leads to life, and only a few find it."—Matthew 7:13-14

Before each of us, two roads are continually being set out. One road, created by Satan, is called "rebellion." He created this road when he rebelled against God in heaven, was cast out and took 1/3 of the angels with him.[36] This road of rebellion is paved with sin and its destination is death, death in every form on earth and in eternity. We can't avoid this road on our own, because we were born into sin. The flesh we live in pulls us toward it. From the first sin committed by Adam and Havah (Eve),[37] mankind has been caught in a trap of sin that separates us from God.[38] However, God has a cure for sin, a way to reconcile us back to Himself: it is His Son, Yeshua the Messiah.[39] Yeshua created the other road called "reconciliation," which is paved with righteousness and leads to life, life eternally with Him and life in its fullest measure here on earth.

Though we have committed ourselves to Yeshua and received Him as Adonai (Lord and Master) over our lives, actually turning over every aspect of ourselves is not as simple as it seems. We may surrender certain areas, but for most of our walk with Him, we continue to withhold parts of our lives, and hearts, from the Messiah. In those areas of our being, we still live off of the desires of our flesh and receive death into ourselves rather than life it is fullest measure. It may not seem like there are areas of our lives full of sin leading to death, because this sin is not as blatant as the sin from which we were first delivered. But everything that is not in God's will for us is sin. Being a believer doesn't make this fact any less true.

The young man Sha'ul (Paul) is an excellent example for us of living off of the desires of our flesh and heading toward destruction. As you will recall, Sha'ul was a religious man. He spent most of his young life in religious training, so he knew the Scriptures forward and backward. And though he lived according to the strictest sect of his religion as a Parush (Pharisee)[40] and was trained by one of the greatest religious leaders of his day,[41] he thrived off of the desires of his flesh. Despite the religious exterior, Sha'ul was a violent man committed to feeding his wrath.

Acts chapter 9 verses 1 and 2 show us how committed to feeding his wrath Sha'ul was. Verse 1 states that he was "still breathing out murderous threats against the Lord's talmidim (disciples)." All of his being was committed to murdering those who served Yeshua. He went out of his way to persecute believers, living off of his wrath, for breath gives us life.[42] What we breathe in brings either life or death into us, and what we breathe out of the storehouse within us gives either life or death to others.[43]

Don't let the Adversary fool you into thinking that there's not something you live for (besides Yeshua), because we all do it and will continue to do it until our transformations into the image of the Messiah are complete. Gluttons live for food. Shoppers live for shopping. Materialists live for money. Control freaks live for control. Violent people live to fight. Cursers live for conflict. Debaters live to prove their points. Dysfunctional rescuers live to protect and care for others. Workaholics live for their work. Broken people live for relationships. Fitness buffs live to work out. The list goes on and on.

Religious Jews and Christians are not excluded. In fact, man-made rules and traditions, disguised as true religion, are designed to mask the flesh into a picture of holiness, giving us a form of godliness without the power of God.[44] Form and fashion without power is dead. Our deliverance doesn't come from religion or religious practices, but rather from the love of God demonstrated through Messiah's sacrifice. He alone can transform us into the people we were created to be and empower us to obey His mitzvot. By mitzvot, I am referring to God's righteous commands found throughout the Bible and given personally to us through the Ruach HaKodesh (Holy

Spirit); these are essential to understanding and fulfilling the will of God for our lives.

When we find ourselves making our own decisions instead of consulting God, guiding our lives through our "wisdom" and experiences, or yielding to other people's wills for us, we're really allowing our sinful desires to rule us. Even if we naturally desire to help others, to improve mankind, and to make a difference in the world, without the Messiah leading us in that effort, we'll eventually find out that we're feeding pride in ourselves, as if we can save anyone through our own efforts. Additionally, we may carry out our "noble intentions" in a manner that is outside of God's will for us. This further demonstrates that the desires of our flesh, without the Messiah to put them in check, will always lead us down a road to destruction.

When we're committed to feeding our flesh, there's nothing anyone, even God, can say to us to change our minds.[45] We rationalize the sins saying, "That's just the way I am," or "That's the way it's been done for years," or my personal favorite, "God knows my heart." At times, we will even find Scriptures to support our desires and "religious" traditions. But hear Yeshua's reply to the P'rushim (Pharisees) in Luke 16:15, "You people make yourselves look righteous to others, but God knows your hearts; what people regard highly is an abomination before God!" Again, ADONAI says in Jeremiah 17:9-10, "The heart is more deceitful than anything else and mortally sick. Who can fathom it? I, ADONAI, search the heart; I test inner motivations; in order to give to everyone what his actions and conduct deserve.'"

As slaves of the Messiah, we should obey His commands at all costs, even at the cost of denying our flesh. In John chapter 8 verse 31, Yeshua addresses the people and says, "If you obey what I say, then you are really my talmidim (disciples), you will know the truth, and the truth will set you free." "Obey what I say" denotes a need to learn what He says (about everything), apply it to our lives and continue in it. Not to read or hear it once, but to hold tight to it throughout life, continuing to receive revelation from it, so that it may set us free as we grow in Him.[46] They replied that they were the seed of Avraham (Abraham) and had never been slaves to anyone, and this is exactly what we say as believers. We deny that we're slaves to sin, as if we were automatically changed into the perfection of the Messiah at the time we received Him without having to exert any effort on our parts. God does miraculously save and deliver us once we submit ourselves, but we have to work with Him in our ongoing transformation into Messiah's image.

    Becoming believers is like joining the military. We can sign our names to the enlistment sheets (confessing the Messiah) and get fitted for the uniform (trying to walk as a believer), but only the transforming experience of bootcamp can make us soldiers. We can identify ourselves with the army and even put on the fatigues, but when it's time to fight, we'll get our tails whipped every time if we skip bootcamp, which consists of our transforming experiences. Even after we've accepted posts as commanders in the army of God, we still have to be trained continually and prepared for upcoming battles because they get longer and fiercer. Otherwise, we will not only allow the enemy to get by us because we failed to recognize him, but we will also allow him the chance to show up in us, causing righteousness to suffer a defeat at our own hands. And yes, both recruits at bootcamp and commanders with years of service are considered part of the army. However, the benefits increase with longevity of faithful service. Additionally, soldiers can be dishonorably discharged from duty at any level of service if they fail to faithfully carry out their duty, denying themselves the right to the retirement plan—and we don't want to miss out on that!

    All of us living, breathing children of God constantly stand in need of transformation. Everything that happens in our lives is a part of God's plan to transform us into the image of His Son. Since you're reading this book, I can tell you with all certainty that it is God's will that you have a transforming experience at this time in your life for He has already begun drawing you toward it. Picking up this book was not a coincidence.

Making Plans Based on Desires

In verses 1 and 2 of Acts chapter 9, we read that Sha'ul requested that he be allowed to leave his country and pursue believers in another country, with the goal of bringing them back to be persecuted in Yerushalayim (Jerusalem). This is a serious commitment to sin. He wanted to wipe the believers off of the face of the earth. He planned his work as a Parush (Pharisee) around this goal. Similarly, we make plans concerning the desires of our flesh. TV junkies schedule their days around their favorite television shows. Fornicators will call in to work sick just to have sex. Egotists won't accept a low-profile job or task even if it's important and needs to be done. People pleasers will alter their plans just to make others happy, no matter how inconvenient or ridiculous the requests.

We all work zealously to fulfill the desires of our flesh. Each time the Messiah reveals to us yet another ruling desire, we can look back on our lives and relationships and see that we have made, and continue to make, major decisions based upon the desires of our flesh. Moreover, we're all plagued with more than one overpowering desire. After God removes one driving desire from us, He then reveals another one that was lying just beneath the first, and so on and so on. Finding that narrow gate to the hard road that leads to eternal life becomes more and more challenging as we develop in our relationship with the Messiah. He doesn't give us more spiritual maturity, wisdom and strength for nothing.

The driving desire we see in our example of Sha'ul is wrath. This wrath consumed his thinking and led him to the road to Damascus, a city in the Roman province of Syria. His journey to Damascus would have taken four to six days done all at once. That didn't bother Sha'ul though; he was on a mission. His mission of murdering the believers led him to make a decision that would've been his downfall. Had he stayed committed to killing all of the believers, he would have missed out on eternity in the presence of the Father. His soul would have perished for this choice.

Just as the road to Damascus was leading Sha'ul to death, being led by our desires in any area of our lives opens us up for death, in some form or another. The alcoholic may get into a fatal car accident, the fornicator may contract HIV, the materialist may squander all of the resources over which God has made her steward, or the person who protects his feelings from getting hurt may push away everyone close to him and be left alone (the very thing he feared most). Your driving desire might not be included in that list, but you still have one.

For example, people pleasing coupled with fear will keep anyone from reaching their potential because they will always be afraid that people won't approve. Being normal is safe, but it will never lead to the fulfillment of God's will for our lives. To truly live life in its fullest measure[47] and walk in the image of the risen Messiah, we all have to let go of our concern for what people think (even religious folk). It's a form of idolatry and will always separate us from God. Only the Messiah can deliver us from this and empower us to be transformed into bold servants of Elohim (Creator) whose only desires are to please the Father.

God loves us so much that He won't allow us to travel too far down any road leading to death without sending Yeshua to warn us. God loved Sha'ul in this same way. His love for Sha'ul was so great that He sent His only Son to appear to the man who desired to kill all of His followers.[48] If God would send His Son to Sha'ul, then He will speak to you again and again to change your heart and your life until you look like the Messiah.

The Need for Deliverance

The Blood of Yeshua atones for our sins; they are henceforth stricken from the record. However, we must continue to grow in Him to stop committing those same sins. Before we came to the Messiah, we attached ourselves to worldly things and unclean spirits. These spirits work to keep us trapped in cycles of sin and make us feel helpless to change. The Spirit of the Holy God is able to drive out every unclean spirit from within us, though. This is called deliverance. I'm not talking about exorcism (though that is a type of deliverance and some of us may need it), but I mean breaking our spiritual ties to Satan.

All of us picked up habits in the world that aren't so easy to let go: cursing, drinking, smoking, fornicating, lying, being lazy, misusing our resources, the list is endless. These habits are linked to unclean spirits. Once we began engaging in sins, we invited the unclean spirits associated with those sins to dwell within us. But these sins, because their outward manifestations are so clearly unbiblical, are fairly easy to spot by us and others, and no religious system will pretend they are godly. Hence, we stop committing those types of sins quickly as believers.

Judgment, pride, commitment to religion over God, self-will, rationalization (which is linked to delusion), and others, however, are much harder to spot because a religiously educated person can make those sins look justified by God's law and holy, much like Sha'ul did. Convincing others that we are not in sin is not the greatest trick of the unclean spirits associated with these sins; the greatest trick is convincing us that we are not in sin. Self-righteousness and fleshly zeal are often used together to conceal and protect these sins within our hearts.

Once these types of sins have found a comfortable place within us, we develop religious practices to feed those unclean spirits. Religious practices, when they become legalistic and traditional, feed our flesh much like sin does because legalism and tradition eliminate the need to inquire of an all-knowing God and submit to His authority at every moment. When we were first called into Adonai's flock, He stripped us of many impurities. We then learned some things that pleased Him and some things that did not, and we developed religious practices from what we learned. Religious practices for a new believer help to keep the flesh in line.[49] The immature need a list of do's and don'ts. Yet, a mature believer is expected to be so connected to the Spirit of God that he is able to discern God's will in all situations and does not need to rely on yesterday's or yesteryear's revelation to please Him.

Yet we must beware: our flesh never leaves us and it would prefer to be in control, rather than submitted to our spirits. Flesh will submit to ritual, because the spirit is not involved, but as we grow in Him, our spirits are expected to mature. We need mature spirits to receive our promised inheritances in the Kingdom of God; I'm not referring to the eternal inheritance, but every blessing and responsibility He has for us in this life.[50]

We can't take manna into the Promised Land.[51] We have to work for our fruit in the Land of the Promise, but it is well worth it because it is giant-sized. Thus, the true indication of whether or not we are ruled by religious practices feeding our flesh or by the Spirit of the Holy God is our fruit.[52] Death can't give life, so dead trees don't produce fruit. When we reach plateaus in our relationship with God or in the ministry to which He has called us, we stop bearing fresh fruit because religion has taken over. Religion will get us by, but it won't let us excel in Him because our spirits won't get fed and we won't have anything to feed others. Lack of nourishment will kill us, and anything attached to us. Remember beloved, God ALWAYS desires for us to learn, grow and change while on this earth. He wants to continually draw us closer to Himself.

Commitment to yesterday's or yesteryear's religious practices over obedience to the voice of God every moment of every day is sin. It's rebellion and idolatry.[53] So as mature believers who desire to go to the next level in God, we must release to Him the practices of our sects, denominations and individual ministries and even the rituals we have developed in our personal relationships with Him. Those practices are based on our spiritual maturity at the time when we began practicing them, and they served us well. However, to move forward, we have to release all of them to Him, so that He can tell us what to keep, what to let go, and what to add.

Once God reveals to us that He desires to take us to a new level and then He begins to show us what we need to surrender to Him in order to go to the next level, it is sinful for us to hold onto those things rather than holding on to God and His commands to us at the time. That is how we turn religion, which was meant to restrain our sinful nature, into idolatry and rebellion, which is sin. Satan doesn't have the power to make us sin, but once we do sin, he seizes the opportunity to trap us into a cycle that will make us powerless over the sin. Hence, commitment to things God clearly wants to change places us in a cycle that can only be broken by God, because we're now in a spiritual stronghold.

Spiritual Strongholds

Whenever we sin continually in the same way and we feel that we can't stop sinning, we're in a stronghold. Through our commitment to sin, an unclean spirit was introduced to us. This spirit then set up residence in our bodies and invited friends. Spirits in a stronghold work together for three very important purposes: 1) to develop our skills in committing those sins, 2) to lock us into downwardly spiraling cycles of sin, and 3) to convince us that they're not there.

"Stronghold" is a term used in times of war. A stronghold is a tightly enclosed and guarded place that no one can get out of and no one can get into. Hence, those spirits literally hold us hostage in our own bodies. They taint all information that comes in to us and all information that comes out from us.[54] Everything we hear, see and otherwise experience is filtered through the stronghold. For example, if you're in a stronghold of arrogance, people might tell you that you're conceited or puffed-up, but that spirit will speak to you inside your head and say, "They're just jealous because they can't be like you." You might even say that out loud in response to people. We don't receive information clearly because the unclean spirit filters out everything that would alarm us to its presence thus putting its home in jeopardy. We'll even say things to protect the spirit inside of us.

Only the Anointed King, who is Yeshua, can reveal to us that we're in a stronghold and in need of deliverance. Yeshua can deliver us from the spirits and transform us into new creatures in those areas. This He'll do continually until we are just like Him. Transformation is then necessary to teach us how to think, feel, act and view the world and ourselves differently, so that we won't return to the state of sin from which we were delivered. Whether we're in a stronghold or just currently warring with one unclean spirit, we'll continue to need deliverance and transformation throughout our journey with the Messiah here on earth. Deliverance and transformation must always go hand-in-hand or we'll return back to our miserable states eventually.[55] If at this point you're thinking to yourself, "I'm not in a stronghold or warring with an unclean spirit," know that the unclean spirit within you just told you that. Just keep praying and reading. God is perfect and a revealer of mysteries.

    I'd like to share a stronghold God delivered me from so that you might see more clearly what I mean. God delivered me from a stronghold of people pleasing years ago—this while I was serving in ministry—and it was a process. The other spirits that I had to be delivered from, so that He could get to the people pleasing, were fear of man, fear of rejection and emotional dependency. God desires for me, and you, to live to please Him, not other people. So, this particular stronghold kept leading me into disobedience, and it was like I couldn't help it. When I had to choose between pleasing people and pleasing God, which happened at least once a day, I often chose to please people, and then I would be mad at myself or them.

    This cycle continued for quite some time until Adonai (the Lord) revealed to me that Satan was keeping me bound in people pleasing with the three spirits listed above. The enemy had discovered that there were some people that I was intimidated by (some of whom were leaders in ministry too), so he used fear of man to keep me in people pleasing. When people opposed me, I would cower before them and give in to their purposes rather than God's. Satan also remembered that I've always wanted to be truly loved and valued by others, so he sent fear of rejection that I might go to any length to maintain relationships with the people in my life, even so far as to please them instead of God. Lastly, emotional dependency sealed the deal by making me believe that my life would be empty and meaningless if certain people didn't fulfill my emotional needs of intimacy and validation. My goal, then, was always to please the people around me, because I was fooled into thinking that I couldn't survive without them.

That stronghold really did a number on my mind and the way I viewed myself. Once those spirits had set in, they opened the door for others like low self-esteem and performance. However, God is really good. He told me the truth: people won't be completely pleased with me no matter what I do, what I desire is just as important as what anyone else desires, and putting anyone before Him in any way is idolatry. When my mind received that, I tried to change, but I was still stuck. So, I confessed my sins and called on Him, and called on Him, and called on Him, until finally He reached His hand from heaven and snatched those spirits from within me. Though I had been in ministry for years, it wasn't until after this deliverance that I was able to truly begin serving God rather than man.[56]

Confession and Submission

Once delivered from evil,[57] I had to be refilled with the Ruach HaKodesh (Holy Spirit). This must happen each time we're delivered. Just as the Father is multifaceted and fills many roles, so is the Ruach HaKodesh (Holy Spirit). I needed to be filled with love and devotion to God; this would lead me to obedience. Then God could begin my transformation that started with teaching me three things: to fear Him alone,[58] that He would never reject me,[59] and to come to Him with every emotional need I had so He could fill it.[60] There was so much more to my transformation in this area (and God's still not done with me), but through this short example, I hope you can see your own need for deliverance in at least one area.

God is faithful to deliver us when we call, but we must do our parts in the deliverance, which you will recall is to confess, submit, accept and repent. Acknowledging our specific sins with our mouths in the presence of God is important in our deliverance because it tears down the strength of the spirits holding us captive. And this is not just a dry statement of our sins. We have to be disgusted with our sins; we must loathe them and describe them thoroughly to God. Delusion is important to the security of those unclean spirits, so when we admit the truth, that we've sinned and we're in a stronghold, much of their defenses are destroyed.

We then must submit ourselves to God so that He can remove the spirits from us. God sometimes commands me to breath out when He's delivering me, sometimes He'll make me vomit and other times wailing is a physical manifestation of my deliverance. However, He chooses to do it, I'm always grateful. Others I know have shared with me that they just feel an overwhelming sense of peace. Who knows how He'll choose to deliver you, just submit yourself to the deliverance, however it happens.

Acceptance and Repentance

The last two steps are often overlooked, and this has devastating affects. Accepting His forgiveness for the sins is essential in our relationship with Yeshua. We receive life in place of death when we believe we are forgiven. Without forgiveness, deliverance loses its keeping power. Let me show you how. If we don't accept that God has forgiven us for the mess that got us into the stronghold, we'll find ourselves back in the same stronghold. Deliverance doesn't mean that we won't sin again, even in that same area. It does mean that when we sin, it'll just be us sinning by choice, not a whole host of spirits pressing us toward the sin. Not accepting Adonai's forgiveness will convince us that we were never delivered in the first place if we sin again. We shouldn't fall unwittingly into the sins that got us into the stronghold of course, but we must recognize that breaking habits takes some time. Additionally, God may command us to do something similar to what we used to do before our deliverance. Yet this time, it's not sin because it's in God's will and timing. But if we don't accept His forgiveness, we won't obey Him when it is His will.

For example, God may deliver someone from glory-hounding, then call him to lead a major movement for the Kingdom. Instead of answering "yes" to the call, he may say "no" for fear that he created the call in order to gain glory for himself or he may just be afraid that glory-hounding will come back if he's in a highly visible position in the Body. Beloved, we must remember how God works. He delivers us from things He knows we can't take with us to the next level. If He delivers someone from glory-hounding, it's because He desires to use that person to bring glory to Himself. When we accept His forgiveness, we receive faith to know that He'll keep us delivered, even when faced with situations in which we would normally sin.

Accepting His forgiveness is essential for us to allow the Messiah to walk with us through the process. Without accepting God's forgiveness, we'll put pressure on ourselves not to do anything resembling that which we confessed (leaning on religion and rules, not God), we'll beat ourselves up if we do sin, and we'll feel helpless all over again, inviting the same spirits back to put us in a stronger stronghold. This trap is called condemnation and it is the opposite of forgiveness, but we'll get into that in detail a little later.

The fourth step in this process, repentance, leads us to transformation. The deliverance doesn't teach us how to turn away from the sins; it just removes the unclean spirits from within us. Yeshua, however, will give us the instructions to turn away from our sins. Then He'll transform us into His image in that area of our being and train us to transform our lives that they will be environments conducive to maintaining our freedom. This once again demonstrates the importance of transformation following EVERY deliverance that believers experience.

Transformation of Believers, then the Body

Often times, we feel that we must transform ourselves into our mental image of a follower of Yeshua. This is always short-lived. We may seem to have it all together, but the truth is that we don't. If we did, we wouldn't need a risen Savior. When we think for a moment that we have mastered this "faith thing," it's then that we need another deliverance from an unclean spirit (in this case, pride) and another transforming experience to keep us clean in that area.

This is particularly true when we serve in ministry. The Messiah is soon to return, and He is transforming His Body into

His image so that we can prepare the world. Hence, our grandparents' religion just won't due. Those practices and teachings that we know so well and use to make those around us feel good inside, well, it's insufficient now. We must always strive to gain clearer revelation of the will of God in these last days. We must then allow the new revelation to transform us personally (in our relationship with God and in our households[61]). Then we are obligated to train others in the new revelation.

That's God's plan for taking the Body back to the power we had in the first century: transforming individual believers who go forth and transform the Body. And the Body really needs transformation. If you don't believe me, consider why liars don't perish in our presence,[62] the dead don't rise at our command,[63] and our shadows don't heal the sick.[64] These are all fruit of a fresh and flourishing relationship with the Father. We don't regularly display this fruit as a Body because are in need of deliverance and transformation, corporately. And that begins with you and me being delivered and transformed, individually.

When God is ready to deliver and transform us in a new area of our lives, He'll start the process all over again for us, in this new area. So, we'll come to another low point and start to feel like things are falling apart or get a nagging feeling that we are incomplete. Then the Messiah will show up and remind us of how much we need Him, we'll have to confess that at our best we're filthy sinners, resubmit ourselves to Him, accept His forgiveness for that area of sin, and allow Him to empower us to repent of it. Being a disciple of the Messiah is like being married, we must wake up everyday and recommit ourselves to the relationship, despite the new challenges and struggles that never fail to come. And just as in a marriage, the only thing that will keep us committed is love—love for God because He first loved us.

The Scriptures are full of filthy sinners who devoted themselves to God and allowed Him to turn their lives around. Such people are often the most zealous and dedicated servants of ADONAI once they commit themselves to a passionate, growing relationship with Him. It's those of us that don't esteem ourselves too highly who can subject ourselves to God as His servants.[65] God has given us a wonderful example of such a transforming experience in a young man named Sha'ul. We'll study his testimony together, so that we might understand the miracle of transformation as we experience it again for ourselves.

CHAPTER 3
DETOURED BY YESHUA

"For he is our God, and we are the people in his pasture, the sheep in his care. If only today you would listen to his voice: 'Don't harden your hearts, as you did at M'rivah, as you did on that day at Massah in the desert, when your fathers put me to the test; they challenged me, even though they saw my work.'"—Psalm 95:7-9

    As children of God, we're Yeshua's family. His desire for His family to be reunited is so strong that He came as a sacrifice to reconcile the relationship severed by our sins.[66] Once brought back into fellowship, He continues to intercede on our behalf until our reunion is complete.[67] Each one of us is in His heart and on His mind, so much so that bringing us into relationship with the Father is His sole mission. He paid the cost for our redemption from death, and, to complete the mission, He continually calls out to each of us personally to make the family whole. The key for us is recognizing the Messiah when He shows up.

    Some of us get to see a vision of Him or hear His voice in our spirits when God desires to deliver us. Others of us experience Yeshua in a different way. It could be through reading or hearing Scripture; it could be through the testimony of someone who went through a similar experience as ourselves; it could even happen through a movie or a book. Regardless of how the Anointed King manifests Himself in your life, your response should be the same as Sha'ul's: humility and fear of God. When I say "fear," I don't mean terror, but respect for His power and might. He has the ability to give life and take it away, so we should take His invitations seriously. He's omnipotent, and extending an invitation to allow Him to straighten up the lives we've messed up is nothing but merciful on His part.

    Verse 3 of Acts chapter 9 lets us know that Yeshua appeared to Sha'ul as he came near to Damascus. So, he was close to fulfilling his desire to persecute the believers there.

Yeshua often shows up just before we do things that will divert us from the path He has set out. He'll give us a feeling that something bad is going to happen though we don't know what, He'll have someone ask us to step down from a position that our souls clearly aren't ready for, or He'll allow something to get in our way like a car breaking down or the alarm clock not ringing. However it happens, Yeshua warns us of the dangerous consequences of our choices and gives us ways out of the sinful situations we've created.[68] It is then up to us to take heed to His warning or continue rebelliously down the road to our destruction.

He Gets Our Attention

When we're on a road to destruction, we're focused on fulfilling our desires in one way or another. God, then, has to do something out of the ordinary to get our attention. The first thing God did to get Sha'ul's attention was to allow a light from heaven to flash around him. This stopped him in his tracks. Similarly, God will do things to get our attention when He desires to transform us. It may be a sudden illness or the absence of His presence; it could be the loss of a job or a drastic change in our lifestyle or financial status; it could even be the introduction of a new and unusual person into our lives. God knows each of us well enough to know what will get our attention.

Being a Parush (Pharisee), Sha'ul was well acquainted with the Scriptures. God knew that Sha'ul would recognize a bright light as a sign from Him. What will it take for you? The answer depends on where you're focused. Sha'ul was focused on getting to Damascus to persecute believers, so Adonai got his attention on the road to Damascus. He'll do the same thing for you. If you're focused on working, it may take the loss of your job to get your attention. If you're focused on your marriage, it might take trouble in your home to get your attention. Now don't misunderstand me, God doesn't plan to unleash misery upon us to get our attention. Instead, He'll just stop protecting us from the natural consequences of our own actions or obstruct our view of the one thing that receives most of our attention.

Respond in Humility

However Adonai chooses to get our attention, it will surely be a humbling experience. It will challenge us in ways we don't want to be challenged, reveal our true character and attack the pride we have in ourselves and our abilities to lead our own lives or ministries. Even the most faithful believers feel somewhere down inside that there are still things that we can handle without ADONAI's guidance. It may not be a conscious thought, but we exhibit this mentality when we fail to consult God or His wisdom in making certain decisions and focus on things or people around us instead of Him and His will for our lives.

Verse 4 of Acts chapter 9 depicts the type of reaction we should have to God's efforts to get our attention: Sha'ul humbled himself. He fell prostrate before Adonai out of his own choosing, not as a result of force or coercion. From what Sha'ul understood of God and the examples in Scripture he had read, this was the respectful reaction to Adonai's presence.[69] He fell to the ground so as not to look upon Yeshua or to appear proud in standing face to face with Him. Once we recognize that God is trying to get our attention, we should humble ourselves before Him, which makes us open to receive from Him. This acknowledges our weakness as mere mortals and God's greatness as the Creator of all things. Then God will speak to us, knowing that we have positioned ourselves to hear what He has to say.

Convicted of Causing Him Pain

Our comfort on our current level often leads us to reject God's call to move to another level in Him. As I've shared with you earlier, this is sin. It's choosing our way, our comfort, over God's way for us. Each new place in Him serves the purpose of getting us to another place. It is all a part of our journey, with the only destination being eternity in His presence. We can never get comfortable on a certain level in our relationships with Him, as if we have "arrived". This leads to complacency, which leads us to rebel against change, and this is sin.

Our sins affect God greatly because He loves us so deeply. His feelings for us are like those of a parent's, only greater. No parent wants to see one of his children stuck in a dead place. We hurt for our children because, in our wisdom and experience, we know that certain behaviors will adversely affect their growth. God knows that our sins lead to death. He knows that we decree death for ourselves, and others, in the 'olam hazeh (this world) and the 'olam haba (the world to come) when we rebel against Him. For this reason, He does whatever He can to stop us from fulfilling our plans to open the way for death. But as He waits for us to acknowledge Him and accept His love and guidance, He grieves over our sins.[70]

In verse 4, Yeshua speaks to Sha'ul and says, "Sha'ul, Sha'ul, why do you keep persecuting me?" This question relays the disappointment and pain that Yeshua felt because of Sha'ul's sins against Him. In other words, He simply asked, "Why do you keep hurting me?" This is the question God poses to all of us after He has gotten our attention on a road to destruction. Our sins hurt His feelings; they're rebellious to Him. Every parent is hurt when his children rebel against him. God even moreso because He not only gave us life, but also continues to provide for us daily, though we fail to respond to His calls in one way or another.

In John 14:15, Yeshua said, "If you love me, you will obey what I command." This is how we express our love to God: we acknowledge that He knows better for us than we know for ourselves, we surrender our will to His will, and we allow His commands to guide our lives. Our rebellion towards Adonai's commands shows Him that we don't truly love Him. When the Messiah shows up on our road to destruction, He places conviction in our hearts for hurting Him by breaking His commands, commands that will take us to a new level in our transformations. This conviction causes us to look at our lives, and ourselves, in a different way. After seeing our sin through the eyes of God, we begin to appreciate His mercy in sending His Son to deliver us once again.

Introduced to Him, Personally

Who is this man who would die for the sins of all of God's children that we might be redeemed from death and brought into the glory of everlasting life? Who is He that would take on the responsibility of turning us back to the Father every time we stray and drawing us closer to God to be more like Him? He is Yeshua the Messiah. "But he was wounded because of our crimes, crushed because of our sins; the disciplining that makes us whole fell on him, and by his bruises we are healed."[71]

After being detoured by Yeshua on a road to destruction, convicted of causing Him pain, and realizing that He's personally invested in our deliverance, we are blessed to get to know Him in yet another way. We may know Yeshua as a Savior or a Teacher, but each time He shows up to rescue us, we come to understand another aspect of His character. It's this intimate knowledge of the Messiah that incites us to submit to His authority and allow Him to change our lives, again and again.

In verse 5 of Acts chapter 9, Sha'ul asks, "Sir, who are you?" Yeshua then introduces Himself to Sha'ul for the first time stating, "I am Yeshua, and you are persecuting me." This was a direct connection between Sha'ul, a guilty sinner, and Yeshua, the Savior of the world. Sha'ul got to see the grace in Yeshua's character. Sha'ul's sins clearly hurt the Messiah, yet He was appearing to him personally. What grace! This is why Sha'ul proclaimed the Good News so fervently for the rest of his life, because he received grace at the hand of the One he had persecuted.

We won't surrender a previously withheld area of our souls to Yeshua as its Master because we remember an aspect of His character from our last encounter with Him. We must have a fresh encounter and learn something new about Him to surrender something new to Him. This encounter may begin the way our other encounters did, but in the end we will know Him more intimately and have a new desire to serve Him. Intimacy with the Messiah is necessary for us to recognize that there is an area in us we have not yet surrendered, receive the revelation that this is God's timing for us to surrender it, then go and tell a dying world about the Savior who delivered us, again.

When Yeshua first introduces Himself to us, we get to know Him as a gentle, loving Deliverer. He doesn't force Himself on us, He doesn't speak harshly to us, but instead He courts us to enter into a love relationship with Him. He extends His hand for us to join Him in wedded bliss, for the Messiah is the Bridegroom and the Body of Believers, His lovely Bride.[72] We soon come to realize that Yeshua has been with us all along, through the good times and the bad, just waiting for us to acknowledge His presence and accept His personal invitation.

After we've accepted the invitation to salvation, we have to continually accept His invitations to deliverance and transformation. Each invitation for deliverance is an invitation to get to know another aspect of His character as He reveals more of our sins to us. When we are in a deep relationship with Him, we often sin against Him because we're not aware that what we are doing is sin and it hurts Him. When He points out a deeper level of sin in us, we get to know Him in a deeper way. Then, through transformation, He implants that newly revealed aspect of His character into our spirits, and we become more like Him.

He Forgives Our Sins

As verse 5 continues, Yeshua identifies Himself to Sha'ul as the One whom he is persecuting. In this statement, Yeshua reveals to him that all of his acts of wrath against the believers were sins directly against the Messiah Himself. Each time we utter a word of cursing instead of blessing, each time we entertain a lustful thought in our minds, each time we direct our lives or service in ministry according to our wills rather than God's, each time we sin, we sin against God. When King David killed Uriyah so that he could have his wife Bat-Sheva (Bathsheba),[73] he was convicted of that sin by a message from God.[74] He then wrote Psalm 51, which includes the following line: "against you, you only, have I sinned."[75] In this statement,

David recognized that all of his sins were against God first. It's God's opinions and feelings that matter, not man's or our own.

When the Anointed King comes to us as a warning to depart from a road to destruction, He identifies Himself as the One against whom we have sinned, but it doesn't end there. The next thing Yeshua immediately does is forgive us and tell us to forgive ourselves. "But get up," is His first command to Sha'ul in verse 6. He didn't command him to stay on the ground; He didn't tell him to wallow in self-pity or condemnation.[76] He told Sha'ul to get up because He had work for him to do. The same is true for each one of us. All the Messiah requires is that we acknowledge our sin before Him. Once we do, He wants us to get up out of that mess and begin to express our love to Him by obeying His commands.

This can be especially difficult when Yeshua reveals to us that our sins have affected others like our families or those we serve in ministry. Often times, going to the next level means cleaning up doctrinal errors and deep character flaws (that made it easy to hold on to the doctrinal errors); both of which affect our families and our service to the Body. It may be a hard pill to swallow to realize that you've been teaching your congregation, Bible study group, women's group or even your children something that is not pleasing to God. Yet, even for those types of sins, Yeshua says, "But get up." He knows all about it and knew that it would happen. In fact, He is wise enough to use even those sins to build character in the people we have misled and even hurt.[77] We just have to confess our sins to Him and those we've misled or hurt, submit to His guidance to make it right, accept His forgiveness and repent by obeying His command to get up and move on . . . on to the next level. Just as our sins affected them, our next-level move will too. He'll let them go with us, those who are willing.

CHAPTER 4
MAKING A U-TURN

"God, in your grace, have mercy on me; in your great compassion, blot out my crimes. Wash me completely from my guilt and cleanse me from my sin."—Psalm 51:1-2

Whenever Yeshua comes to detour us from a path to destruction, we must consciously decide to leave that path. Our sins separate us from God, even those unknown to us, so we have to bring ourselves back to Him once we are made aware. The Messiah provided the way back to the Father and keeps extending invitations for reconciliation. Yet we must accept each invitation and walk down the road of reconciliation, which you will recall is paved with righteousness and leads to life—life eternally with Him and life in its fullest measure on earth. Each time Yeshua reveals our sin to us and we respond by allowing Him to transform us, we get closer to the narrow path to life that was set out for us before we were born. Because sin in any form leads to a corresponding form of death, we can't continue to sin if we desire to have life in its fullest measure.

We're not expected to turn away from sins we're not aware that we commit. However, once the Savior shows up and reveals those sins to us, we should then be moved to allow God to change our hearts and empower us to make different choices. "'Therefore house of Isra'el, I will judge each of you according to his ways,' says Adonai ELOHIM (The Lord GOD). 'Repent, and turn yourselves away from all your transgressions, so that they will not be a stumbling block that brings guilt upon you. Throw far away from yourselves all your crimes that you committed, and make yourselves a new heart and a new spirit; for why should you die, house of Isra'el [insert your name there]? I take no pleasure in the death of anyone who dies,' says Adonai ELOHIM (the Lord GOD), 'so turn yourselves around, and live!'"[78]

Forgiveness Leads to Obedience

Remember in chapter 1, Yeshua said, "Because of this, I tell you that her sins—which are many!—have been forgiven, because she loved much. But someone who has been forgiven only a little loves only a little."[79] He was, of course, speaking of the sinful woman who anointed His feet with perfume in comparison to the self-righteous Parush (Pharisee). In this example, the Messiah makes a clear connection between being forgiven and loving Him. We fall deeper in love with Yeshua as we realize how willing He is to forgive our foulness in sinning. The more sins we acknowledge before Him, the more sins He forgives, and the more we love Him for it. As we grow as believers, the Messiah reveals more and more sins to us. Thus, our love for Him should constantly increase, and it should be demonstrated in our increasing obedience to His commands.

Yeshua's second command to Sha'ul, in Acts 9 verse 6, was to "go into the city, and you will be told what you have to do." Sha'ul was obedient to His instructions and was led into the city by his companions on the road. Yeshua had forgiven much, so Sha'ul loved much and demonstrated this in his obedience. Remember, obedience is an expression of our love for the Messiah.[80] Don't allow yourself to be fooled into thinking you can accept Yeshua's deliverance without being obedient to His commands after the deliverance. Our acts of disobedience point out areas of our lives that we've not allowed Him to rule and invite unclean spirits to enter or, in this case, return.

For example, after I was delivered from people pleasing, I was still disobedient to God's call to minister to the children of Isra'el. This showed me that people pleasing wasn't the only reason I had not accepted that call. I still needed to be delivered from insecurity, which is a form of pride because it focuses on my inability instead of His omnipotent ability to work through me. That's why transformation is a continuous process. Every time the Messiah forgives us, we get to know Him in a new way, our love for Him increases, we become obedient in a new area of our lives, and we're transformed into His likeness in that area. Transformation is not a fast or easy process, so God continues to send us everything we need so that our transformations will be complete.[81]

The Scripture makes it clear that Sha'ul needed help to be obedient. His companions had to lead him into Damascus because he was blind. In the same way, we need help when the Messiah calls us to obedience in a new area of our lives. Like Sha'ul, we can't see the way before us clearly without the help of other believers. It's a trap to be proud and think that we can obey Yeshua without help from anyone else. This lie will cause us to return to our old sins, or that old comfortable level, in the blink of an eye. Building relationships with other believers will help sustain us in our transformations. In my example above, God placed some compassionate and anointed Messianic Jews in my life who revealed more of the truth of the Bible to me and increased my faith in God to use me to minister to His people Isra'el alongside them. In fact, my brothers and sisters revealed to me that it has been God's plan from the beginning to make Jewish and Gentile believers one and draw all Isra'el back to Himself.[82]

A Repentant Heart

In verse 17 of Psalm 51, King David writes, "My sacrifice to God is a broken spirit; God, you won't spurn a broken, chastened heart." David's repentance of adultery and murder included being broken. His pride and lust led him to commit adultery with Uriyah's wife. His desire to hide his sin led him to murder one of his warrior-heroes, a leader in his army.[83] David had to turn away from those sins—adultery, murder and deceit—in order to repent before God. Since it was his pride and lust that led him to the sin, he had to be broken in order to turn away from it to God.

Pride leads us to all conscious sins. Were we completely humble, we would never intentionally rebel against God. Hence, being broken before God surrenders our pride, which caused us to depart from Him in the first place. In doing so, we acknowledge our wrongdoing and accept the consequences of our sins. Even in cases where we unwittingly committed sins, we must still be broken in order to willingly allow Him to demolish and reconstruct areas in our hearts and lives.

If we truly love God, our hearts will grieve over the grief we cause Him. This doesn't mean that we'll condemn ourselves or even punish ourselves,[84] for there is nothing we can do to atone for our sins. Only pride would make us think that we can atone for sins in and of ourselves; we can make reparations, which means to try to repair some of the damage we've done, but we can never make it right. The Messiah was and is the atonement for sin, so we must accept forgiveness from Him.[85] Our passionate love for God, however, will cause us to be sorry for our actions. That godly sorrow[86] comes from a chastened, or repentant, heart.

Sha'ul had a broken spirit and a chastened heart after his encounter with Yeshua. Verse 9 of Acts chapter 9 reads, "For three days he remained unable to see, and he neither ate nor drank." Sha'ul fasted and prayed for three days straight while he was blind. He used his time of affliction to call out to God and become closer in relationship with Him. Prayer opens up the line of communication with God. So when we pray, we should acknowledge our sins, thank God for His forgiveness and ask that our spiritual needs be met. Because fasting denies our flesh, it increases our ability to connect with God in our spirits and receive His Ruach HaKodesh (Holy Spirit).

Refusing to eat for three days was a sacrifice to Sha'ul's body,[87] not done as a penance,[88] but for cleansing and spiritual healing. He had committed many sins against God and expressed his sorrow for those sins while being purged of the evil with which he'd allied himself. We open ourselves up to the Adversary when we sin, whether knowingly or unknowingly. Fasting and praying are tools that God has given us to help destroy our relationship with the Adversary and break his connection to us.[89]

Avoiding the Trap of Condemnation

Confessing our sins to God is an important element in our daily prayers to break our ties with Satan. We must fast as well to avoid Satan's trap for us when we acknowledge our sins. He knows that we need to acknowledge our sins to God[90] and to each other[91] in order to clear our consciences and receive Adonai's forgiveness into our hearts. He also knows that this open confession of sins, which leads to forgiveness, will strengthen our love for God. So, he uses a trap called condemnation to get us off of the road of reconciliation and back onto the road of rebellion.

Satan, which means "accuser", will continually beat us over the heads with our sins to condemn us. That's the opposite of forgiveness. God will send conviction into our hearts when we sin, so that we'll acknowledge the sin before Him. We should, however, immediately receive God's forgiveness into our hearts if we're truly repentant. If we instead receive condemnation into our hearts, especially after we've confessed and repented, that didn't come from God; it came from Satan. We then turn from the road of reconciliation back to the road of rebellion. This happens because we confuse Satan with God, thinking that ADONAI hasn't forgiven us. So, we literally feel "damned if we do, and damned if we don't." Anyone who feels this way is going to rebel because working hard to improve seems meaningless.

That's why receiving God's forgiveness into our hearts is so important. Only then can we understand His true love for us and be empowered to love Him back, which leads to obedience. Beloved, don't let the Adversary fool you into thinking that condemnation comes from God, whether it comes to you from your spouse, friends, family members, brothers and sisters in the faith, or even a spiritual leader. All God requires is that we confess our sins and allow Him to cleanse us and change us.

Acknowledging that we have sinned also includes acknowledging that we don't know how to stop sinning.[92] Whenever we submit to the belief that we can stop committing ANY type of sin without God's help, we're setting ourselves up for condemnation. Our relationship with God is based upon His grace and mercy, not our ability to live holy. We CAN'T live holy; our flesh won't allow it. We can pretend to be righteous for a little while, but sin will ALWAYS come back if we don't submit ourselves to God continually.[93]

For this too, we have a wonderful example in Sha'ul. He never allowed condemnation to keep him from serving Adonai. People often reminded him that he had persecuted believers,[94] but he knew that he had been cleansed with the blood of the Messiah. We too must stand firm as Sha'ul did, confident not in ourselves, but in the One whom we have believed. Yeshua is capable of working through us despite our past and even present sins. As long as we regularly surrender those sins to Him, through confession and repentance, He will forgive us and continue to develop us into the people we were created to be.

Sha'ul helps to explain our powerlessness over sin in Romans chapter 7, verses 14 through 25. However, Sha'ul goes on in Romans 8:1-4 to state,

> "Therefore, there is no longer any condemnation awaiting those who are in union with the Messiah Yeshua. Why? Because the Torah (Law) of the Spirit, which produces this life in union with Messiah Yeshua, has set me free from the 'Torah' (Law) of sin and death. For what the Torah (Law of Moses) could not do by itself, because it lacked the power to make the old nature cooperate, God did by sending his own Son as a human being with a nature like our own sinful one [but without sin]. God did this in order to deal with sin, and in so doing he executed the punishment against sin in human nature, so that the just requirement of the Torah (Law of Moses) might be fulfilled in us who do not run our lives according to what our old nature wants but according to what the Spirit wants."

It is the Ruach HaKodesh (Holy Spirit), whom we receive when we accept salvation through Yeshua,[95] who empowers us to stop sinning. Sha'ul was able to proclaim this boldly because He knew that the Messiah had forgiven him and would continue to cleanse him of all unrighteousness.

God loves us, and He is waiting for us to give Him the opportunity to forgive our sins. Not only does ADONAI desire to forgive us, but He also wants to give us instructions for staying clean in those areas of our lives. Often times, we don't receive instructions from God because we're too connected to our flesh and not connected enough to His Ruach (Spirit). Our flesh not only prevents us from living holy, but it also allows condemnation to attack us for not living holy. That's another good reason to fast; it subjects our flesh to the Ruach HaKodesh (Holy Spirit) within us. Once our flesh is brought into submission to the Ruach (Spirit), the voice of condemnation is silenced and we can receive the instructions we need to leave the road of rebellion and get on the right track to life, here and in eternity.

Acts of Tzedakah (Righteousness)

The Adversary is so tricky in the way he works against us that he'll use the very thing that we believe we're supposed to do, to get us off the road to life and back onto the road to death. Satan has dispatched a lie to God's children everywhere that we can earn life by charitable acts, living holy or serving in ministry—acts of tzedakah (righteousness). The ONLY way to receive life in eternity and here on earth, which we can never earn, is to submit to Yeshua the Messiah as Adonai and Deliverer.

There is nothing in us, apart from His Ruach (Spirit), that can transform us into the people God created us to be. We will always fall short, and one sin makes us unworthy of living in His presence.[96] As children of El 'Elyon (God Most High), we have to stop trying to attain life through our own strength and allow the Messiah to transform us piece by piece. Proverbs 20:21 states, "An inheritance quickly gained at the beginning will not be blessed in the end" (NIV). This inheritance of life—life with God forever[97] and life in its fullest measure on earth[98]—is too precious for us to try to receive through our normal "get rich quick" schemes. There is no shortcut, no easy way, to be transformed into the likeness of the Messiah; we just have to allow God to do it. He made us, and He's got to change us through the Messiah.

We're called "believers" as opposed to "workers" because our relationship with God is based upon our belief, or faith, in Him.[99] That's how we are saved, not by our works, or acts of tzedakah (righteousness). God's natural order of things is to begin with our minds, move on to our hearts, then our spirits, then our bodies. Hence, our minds must first conceive of the idea that a perfect God can and does forgive filthy sinners like us. Then our hearts will begin to love Him for that and submit to Him. Next, we will receive another aspect of His Ruach (Spirit) into our spirits to transform us. Lastly, our bodies will be empowered to act in obedience to God's will.

Throughout history, Satan has always done the same thing: copy God's ways and pervert them because he is not and cannot be holy. Thus, he operates in a similar manner. He convinces our minds that God has not and will not forgive us (condemnation). Then he turns our hearts to despise God, and possibly ourselves or others, because we believe that God expects too much from us or leaves us just when we need Him. Next, he sends unclean spirits to reside in us and lock us into spiritual strongholds. Lastly, these spirits incite us to behave rebelliously toward God with our bodies because we believe we're going to hell anyway, so why keep fighting the good fight.[100]

We allow Satan to trap us into condemnation when we try to skip acknowledging our sins, receiving God's forgiveness and loving Him and, instead, go straight to serving His people. Without confession, forgiveness and love for God, our service and charitable acts are self-serving and proud because they're not led by God. Hence, they won't bear the giant-sized fruit that comes from true obedience (as we explored in chapter 2), and we'll feel that God has neither seen nor honored our "obedience", and thus turn our hearts from a seemingly uncaring Father.

It takes the mind of the Messiah[101] to see the Adversary at work here because he's tricky. Only submission to God empowers us to resist the devil.[102] His trap to get us to skip confession, forgiveness and love (which all come through submission) and perform acts of tzedakah or religious practices instead is another way to get us off the road to life back onto the road to destruction. Thus, trying to earn life based upon acts will always set us up to feel and be condemned.

Look at Yeshua's example of the P'rushim (Pharisees) in Matthew chapter 6. He discusses their acts of tzedakah (righteousness), and He states that they will not receive a reward from the Father in heaven because they have received their reward here on earth, which is honor from men. In chapter 23 of Matthew, Yeshua again calls them hypocrites and points out that their claims to be righteous are false, because they haven't allowed God to clean them on the inside. To demonstrate this, Yeshua uses an example in verses 25 and 26 about a cup and a dish. He states that the inside must be cleaned first; then the outside will be clean.

We too must be cleaned by God on the inside; then we'll be able to display our cleanness through our outward actions, thus bearing fruit. As God takes us to new levels in our relationships with Him, we must allow Him to genuinely transform us first before we try to bear fruit on those levels. Not doing so will always set us up for condemnation, because we won't bear fruit that will last. Then, we'll become confused and blame God, thus leading us back to the comfort of our old level, which is rebellion toward His call to move onward and upward.

Instructions for Repentance

Yeshua's love for us will not only lead Him to forgive us, but also to give us direction as to how we can remain clean and not return to the sins His blood has washed away.[103] This direction includes our specific instructions for repentance, which you will recall means to turn away from our sins to God. In order to receive these instructions, God will often lead us to places where there are other believers. They may explain repentance to us, they may deliver the instructions for our repentance, or they may serve as a support system for us as we turn from our sins to God. Changing behaviors we've held on to and justified for years is not an easy process. Believers need each other, because our flesh will always resist change. Other Messianic believers and Christians can guide us through Scripture and give us practical advice about living out God's words on a daily basis.

As you will recall, Yeshua instructed Sha'ul to go into Damascus because he would be told what to do there. Damascus, the city in which Sha'ul planned to persecute believers, was the place Yeshua sent Sha'ul to be guided and cared for by believers. Sha'ul stayed at the house of a believer named Y'hudah (Judas), who lived on Straight Street, while he was blind those three days. Hananyah (Ananias), another believer who lived in Damascus, was sent to Y'hudah's (Judas') house to be used in Sha'ul's healing, to give Sha'ul his instructions for repentance and to prepare him to carry them out. Had Sha'ul not allowed himself to be cared for by the believers in Damascus, out of pride, fear, guilt or any other reason, he wouldn't have been healed nor reconciled to God.

When Yeshua calls to Hananyah (Ananias) and tells him to go to Sha'ul in verse 11, He adds that Sha'ul is praying. He continues in verse 12, "and in a vision he has seen a man named Hananyah (Ananias) coming in and placing his hands on him to restore his sight." As a result of Sha'ul's commitment to seeking God through prayer and fasting, he received a vision about his healing. God desires to speak to us and give us instructions. Often times, we don't receive these instructions because we're not listening or our spirits are disconnected from His. Don't be mistaken though; there are certain things God chooses not to reveal or waits to reveal, because He knows all. As flawed humans, too much revelation can cause us to move ahead of God and disrupt His plans.

Obedience to Adonai's instructions after encountering Him is essential to our transforming experience. An encounter with Yeshua is not enough to change us from sinner to servant. This is made evident by the religious leaders' reactions to Him during the time of His earthly ministry. They had encounters with Him, but they rejected Him as the Messiah and refused to obey His teachings. If we fall into the same trap, we won't live with Him eternally. Yeshua knows exactly what it will take to transform us into His likeness, so we must receive Him and obey.

Our repentance is based on the sins from which the Messiah has delivered us. He fully expects that after each personal encounter with Him, we will receive His power to change our behaviors and our lives so as not to be caught up in the same sins. This takes active participation and hard work on our parts. Sha'ul persecuted believers; repentance for him included creating more believers through proclaiming the Good News. Yeshua shares this with Hananyah (Ananias) after he objects to going to Sha'ul to be used in his healing. In verse 15, Yeshua says, "Go, because this man is my chosen instrument to carry my name to the Goyim (Gentiles), even to their kings, and to the sons of Isra'el as well." After being immersed (baptized) and filled with the Ruach HaKodesh (Holy Spirit), Sha'ul was faithful in carrying out these instructions as we see in verses 20 through 22 of Acts chapter 9.

First John 3:5-6 reads, "You know that he appeared in order to take away sins, and that there is no sin in him. So, no one who remains united with him continues sinning; everyone who does continue sinning has neither seen him nor known him." This Scripture doesn't mean that we will immediately become perfect, but rather that we will make the changes God calls for when He points out our sins to us. No one who loves God will ignore His instructions for repentance in their lives. It's true that we're not able to carry out these instructions, in and of ourselves, but we must ask for His help and believe that God is capable of strengthening us.[104]

Chapter 5
Walking With Adonai
-Markita's Testimony-

"'Briefly I abandoned you, but with great compassion I am taking you back. I was angry for a moment and hid my face from you; but with everlasting grace I will have compassion on you,' says ADONAI your Redeemer."
—Isaiah 54:7-8

Yeshua has always been close to me, but most of my life I was disconnected from Him. My mother often shares the story of hearing from God in the hospital room after I was born that He wanted to use me in His service. She learned shortly thereafter that my grandfather heard the same thing. She prayed hard for me then and has not stopped praying. God placed good people around me to guide me and pray for me, but it was years before I really started praying for myself. I went through phases of joining churches and coming on Sundays for worship service, I would even serve God briefly during those phases. However, I was not fully surrendered to His will for my life, so my service was always short-lived. After a few months, I would return to my state of inactivity in the Body, which included attending church on holidays, rarely reading my Bible and only praying out of habit or need. I was not a tither[105] and gave only $1.00 for an offering whenever I did attend service. That is, until the Savior stepped in.

Despite my complacency as a believer and lack of fruitfulness for the Kingdom,[106] I've always been able to hear the voice of God. He has always been near to me, protecting me, guiding me and loving me in an extraordinary way. He would tell me which choices to make so that I wouldn't get hurt, He would allow doors to just open up for me at school and at work, He even answered questions I had through Scripture. It was so natural to me that I thought everyone in the world experienced Him as I did.

However, one day God stopped talking, just like that. It was like going to sleep with the TV on; you're not really paying attention to it, but if someone turns it off, you wake up because the silence is so abrupt. I asked Him why He had left me, and He sent sermons about fornication and gave me Scriptures about fornication[107], but I ignored them because I was so committed to my justifications for having sex outside of marriage. I even wrote the Scriptures down so that I could share them with other people I thought needed them. That's how blind I was to my own sin.

As a young girl, I was always an obedient child and student. However, I began to dabble in dating relationships at an early age. Though my parents told me I couldn't have a boyfriend until I was 13, I began spending time with a boy I "liked" in second grade. Our parents knew each other, through us, and so we would eat dinner at each others' houses and go to the movies. My little friend was very nice; he came from a good family and his father was a pastor. He was such a gentleman; he even gave me gifts. But a few weeks later, I met another boy. He was the "bad boy" type. I started to like him more, and dumped my other friend, publicly, at school.

After that incident, I continued to "like" boys and spend time with them. It all seemed pretty innocent, nothing risqué or sexual. But when I was bored with them, I cut them off abruptly. This behavior continued into my adult years. Though I was always very nice, I was fickle and disloyal. I broke quite a few hearts. One in particular belonged to a young man who asked me to marry him during my senior year in high school. He was two years older than I and mature enough to ask the question. I, however, was not mature enough to answer it. To make matters worse, his proposal came at a time when I was emotionally devastated because my father had just left home again. Though I knew I should say "no", I accepted his proposal only to break up with him a few months later.

While breaking up with little boys who liked me may not seem like much of a sin, breaking my promise to a young man, after accepting his proposal for marriage and allowing him to be my first sexual partner, demonstrates that the traits I had been exhibiting all along were, in fact, sinful. As I reflect over those years (from second grade on), I realize that my hurtful behavior set me up for a pattern of unhealthy relationships. Whenever I would finally find a young man I truly cared for, he would always treat me the way I had treated the young men I dumped. This downwardly spiraling cycle, brought on by my unchecked character flaws, set me on a path that drastically changed the course of my life.

Then, another damaging element was added. As a little girl, I always wanted to be attractive. I had a lovely face, but in 5th grade I felt like a late bloomer. In the summer before I entered 6th grade though, God answered my prayers and my body matured, almost overnight. The only problem was that this caused me to get attention from everywhere, even undesirable places. In middle and high school, I had trusted men in my life (counselors and mentors) touch me in appropriately. I had boyfriends and other acquaintances sexually assault me. During my freshman year in college, a friend of mine violently raped me, and I determined at that moment that something was wrong with me, and I had to change. I started to devalue my body, to numb myself to the pain of defilement, and I became the predator instead of the prey. This led to a year of promiscuity in college, further damaging my self-image and my ability to cultivate healthy romantic relationships.

I think a lot of people turn to things outside of themselves for comfort when they're in pain: partying, drugs, relationships, food, shopping, whatever. And that's just what I did. I turned to sex for comfort in my pain, and opened myself up to a series of behaviors and rationalizations that transformed me into a person I hardly recognized. At first, I only had sex in monogamous relationships. Then I began to feel more comfortable with casual sex. My heart was never really into that though, so every now and then I would be celibate for a while. However, I would always allow my flesh to overpower me and return to fornication.

Sex became my comforter, my stress reliever, and a way to escape from the world for a moment. Fornication, coupled with my fickle and disloyal character, plunged me deeper and deeper into a pit of sin until I reached a point where

I had let go of most of my standards in relationships. My concept of womanhood and self-esteem became so warped that taking pride in myself turned into pride in my body and the reactions I could get from it. I was in bondage to sin and unable to escape. So, during my junior year in college, in an attempt to save myself from sin, I decided to get married.

My first marriage failed miserably because I didn't consult God at all and I thought I could address my sin by myself. I tried to fulfill what I thought were the responsibilities of a wife, and I worked very hard to keep myself from having contact with other men, to make sure that I wouldn't be tempted. I successfully suppressed the lust in me, but then I had to address the other problems I had in relationships. I loved my husband and we were best friends, but I realized that neither of us was ready to get married. So, my fickle and disloyal nature showed up again (but this time with justification, or so I thought), and I asked him to move out.

After being separated for a year, I began to date a young man with whom I fell in love. He and I had a sexual relationship, which I justified in my mind because we weren't seeing anyone else. It was during this relationship, shortly after my divorce was finalized, that God took His presence away from me to get my attention. One evening, after receiving the sermons and Scriptures about fornication, I was lying awake in my bed and asked again why He had left me. He answered me by whispering one word, "Fornication." In that moment, God allowed me to feel the pain I had caused Him with every sinful sexual act. My spirit mourned, I wept and I felt so ashamed. I had no idea my sins hurt Him so deeply, so personally.

The next morning, I promised God that I would never fornicate again. He told me, "It is better not to make a vow than to make a vow and break it."[108] I later understood why He had said this to me. My tendency to break covenants was yet unaddressed. I slept with my boyfriend a few more times after that, because I was powerless to deliver myself from sin. God had to do it, and one night, He showed up. I could actually feel His eyes watching me, and I couldn't do it. I said "no" to my boyfriend for the first time and committed myself to celibacy.

The young man and I then drifted apart because he couldn't handle being celibate and wasn't ready to get married.

For the next few months, I prayed and read the Bible everyday. Yeshua and I spent real quality time together. He then led me to Isaiah chapter 54, which He used to tell me that He was my Husband.[109] It was like reading a love poem from God. In it, ADONAI speaks of Yerushalayim as if the city were an abandoned woman. That's why the chapter meant so much to me because that was how I felt. I was ashamed about how my marriage ended. I felt like God had left me, but that chapter was His promise to me that He would never leave me again. He loves ME, specifically and personally. No man has ever, will ever, make me feel like that. To be romanced by God, there is nothing like it.

I then got the call to minister[110] and soon after a call to prophesy,[111] but I didn't know what to do. I had never thought about working for Yeshua. My whole life I had planned to work for myself and help some people along the way, but serving in the Body of the Messiah never crossed my mind. So, God led me to contact a minister at my family church, and I shared my call with her. She invited me to worship service, and I immediately began working in the children's ministry and became reinstated as a member.

God spoke to me everyday, and I served Him diligently. Then the Ruach HaKodesh (Holy Spirit) started to come upon me in power.[112] At first, it only happened during my quiet time with ADONAI. He would speak to me and then blanket me with His Spirit. I could actually feel Him moving all through me, from my toes to my head, even in my fingertips. It was indescribably wonderful, being filled to the brim with God's unchanging love. Later on, I began to receive the Ruach HaKodesh (Holy Spirit) while at church as well. I even prophesied at my church. This was the beginning of my walk with Him. Not long after, God called me to go on missions trips,[113] and I joined another church. Three years later, God brought forth a ministry through me called The Truth In The Spirit, and He called me to be His emissary (aka apostle)[114]. I still lead this ministry with my husband, and this year we will celebrate the ministry's 18th anniversary.

Yeshua has empowered me to be the wife, mother, minister and entrepreneur God planned for me to be before the foundations of the earth. That feeling of brokenness I experienced after He revealed my sin of fornication to me is a feeling I experience regularly, because I am still not holy or righteous enough to serve Him or represent Him to His people. Yet, in His grace, He continually sends His Son to deliver me from newly revealed areas of sin in my heart, He washes me white as snow through Yeshua's blood, and teaches me to begin again, each time on a new level of my relationship with Him and with a new level of anointing to serve His people.

PART II
TRANSFORMED INTO THE MESSIAH'S IMAGE

"Therefore, if anyone is united with the Messiah, he is a new creation—the old has passed; look, what has come is fresh and new!"

2 Corinthians 5:17

Chapter 6
Immersed

"It's true that I am immersing you in water so that you might turn from sin to God; but the one coming after me is more powerful than I—I'm not worthy even to carry his sandals—and he will immerse you in the Ruach HaKodesh (Holy Spirit) and in fire."—Matthew 3:11

All of us experience times in our lives when something significant occurs and it completely changes us. We know that after that event or occurrence we will never be the same. Some of these events are planned solely by God, and usually we're caught off guard by them. I call these "God sightings", because it's as if the Almighty parts the heavens and comes down to earth just to make changes in our lives. Other life-changing events are planned by us and others around us, such as starting a career or getting married.

Whether God initiates the change or we do it ourselves, life-changing moments tend to serve as rites of passage for us. They transition us from one chapter of our lives to another one. We may not have a formal ceremony, like a wedding, or create a spiritual marker, like Y'hoshua (Joshua) did when the children of Isra'el crossed over the Yarden (Jordan) River,[115] but we are prepared to leave one way of life in exchange for another one.

When young people graduate from high school, they have lots of choices to make. They can choose to enter the workforce, they can go to college, they can get married or they can stay home with mom and dad and loaf around their house (which, by the way, is a poor choice). However, returning to high school is NOT an option. There are laws against that. Adults can't just sit in classes with minors or hang around school buildings. Sure, they're only a year older than the rising seniors, but they're now in a different demographic group. They have legal rights, like the right to vote, and they have legal authority to stand as independent people, no longer needing their parents to sign off on things for them. They can get credit, make major purchases, and make other decisions that will affect them for years to come. Thus, their senior year in high school should prepare them for life as an adult, because adulthood, with all of its responsibilities, is coming whether the graduates are ready for it or not.

Immersion is the process of submerging something into something else so as to cover it up completely. In the Old and New Covenants (Testaments), the children of Isra'el immersed themselves in water and continue to do so today. This process is not a dipping or dropping of water onto one person by another person. Instead, individuals surrender themselves completely before God and immerse themselves into water to symbolize spiritual purification. Because Yeshua Himself was immersed in this manner and this is the way it was performed throughout the Bible, I will use the term "immersion" rather than "baptism". In so doing, we will allow the Ruach HaKodesh (Holy Spirit) to take us back to Scripture and God's original intent for immersion.

Just as the senior year for high school students is a year of preparation and transition, immersion serves to prepare and transition believers into the next level in the Messiah. Thus, believers may be immersed as often as the Ruach HaKodesh (Holy Spirit) directs. Whether it's immersion in water, the Ruach HaKodesh or fire—which is suffering—we'll always be reminded that God has changed us forever. Yeshua Himself was immersed in all three,[116] and we're called to follow in His footsteps.[117] Now it's true, immersion, in any form, can't save us; only the Blood of Yeshua can. However, immersion brings us closer to ADONAI and purifies us for His service. Our model, Yeshua didn't conform Himself to religious practices or formalities.[118] The Messiah limited Himself to that which was pleasing to His Father,[119] which demonstrates for us the significance of immersion.

To understand the importance of immersion in the life of a believer, we may also look back at our Biblical example in the young Parush (Pharisee), Sha'ul. Verses 15-19 of Acts chapter 9 show us that Sha'ul was, in fact, immersed in water, the Ruach HaKodesh (Holy Spirit) and fire. When calling Hananyah (Ananias) to be used in Sha'ul's healing, Yeshua says to him, "Go, because this man is my chosen instrument to carry my name to the Goyim (Gentiles), even to their kings, and to the sons of Isra'el as well. For I myself will show him how much he will have to suffer on account of my name." This was a foretelling of Sha'ul's fire immersion. As Hananyah (Ananias) entered the house in which Yeshua told him he could find Sha'ul, he placed his hands on him and said, "Brother Sha'ul, the Lord—Yeshua, the one who appeared to you on the road as you were coming here—has sent me so that you may see again and be filled with the Ruach HaKodesh (Holy Spirit)." This was Sha'ul's immersion in the Ruach HaKodesh. After the scales fell from Sha'ul's eyes, he was then immersed in water.

Immersion in Water

When God's people Isra'el and Messianic believers are immersed, we wash ourselves thoroughly first. Every inch of our bodies and hair is cleaned, nails are trimmed to be sure no dirt remains, and anything that would prohibit a part of our body from being drenched in the waters is removed. Thus, the immersion itself does not serve the purpose of physical cleansing. That part has already occurred prior to immersion. The water immersion, instead, is a spiritual submission to God to make us holy as He is.

A person being immersed presents herself before God without any physical barriers, which represents the removal of all spiritual barriers in her relationship with Him. Hence, those being immersed are either totally naked or loosely covered to be sure that the water touches every part of the body. When a person is immersed, no other person touches her. That would be a barrier between the person being immersed and God. Instead, she surrenders herself and submerges herself completely in high water to insure that every part of her body is completely covered.

For a moment, she feels weightless in a completely new environment. This symbolizes the change that occurs within her spirit and in her life. During the brief moments of the actual immersion, she is suspended in water and totally helpless in her environment like a baby in the womb. And much like the womb experience, water immersion is preparation for birth into a new life, a life of total dependence on God, which is necessary to thrive in the new environment of the next level she will step into after the immersion.

Yochanan the Immerser (John the Baptist) immersed in water and Yeshua in the Ruach HaKodesh (Holy Spirit) and fire,[120] yet before Yeshua began His ministry, He went to Yochanan (John) to be immersed in water. This was Yeshua's submission to the will of the Father for the next, and last, three years of His life on earth. He was then filled with the Ruach HaKodesh, as Yochanan saw it descend upon Him like a dove, and led into the desert to begin His immersion in fire. God also testifies to Yochanan (John) that Yeshua is His Son, but only after Yeshua accepted His call and was immersed in water before man and God.[121]

With this knowledge, it's clear why Yeshua allowed Himself to be immersed before beginning His earthly ministry. He may not have needed purification from sins, but He did need to demonstrate for us that before we begin any great endeavor in the Name of God, we must surrender to Him completely, making us totally dependant on Him to take us to a place we have never been.

Water immersion is like a wedding ceremony. For most of us, planning a wedding is more than planning a ceremony. Many things occur to actually prepare the couple for marriage, rather than just for the event of their "big day". The rabbi or minister who has agreed to perform the service gives premarital guidance. The families of the bride and groom meet (if they have not already) and continually offer advice and support to the couple. Preparations are also made to insure that the couple will have an income and place to live after the wedding. Then the day comes when they make vows to one another before man and God. From that day on, they are no longer considered two separate people, but one unit.

In a similar way, preparation is necessary for every new level to which God desires to take us. Much like the marriage and wedding preparations, the preparations for immersion are both physical and spiritual, with long-lasting spiritual implications. So, at the time of immersion, the person being immersed is prepared to surrender himself to God for removal of all that doesn't need to be taken to the next level. The water immersion is like the wedding ceremony, a beautiful outward expression that culminates much physical and spiritual preparation and marks the end of an era in our lives and the beginning of a new one.

Since immersion in water represents the wedding, immersion in the Ruach HaKodesh (Holy Spirit) represents the honeymoon. God consummates His relationship with us by depositing a part of Himself into us: the Ruach HaKodesh. The Ruach HaKodesh connects us to God and transforms us into His likeness. This makes water immersion all the more important because we must be prepared for what God will deposit into us for our next level transformation. The preparations for water immersion empty us to receive completely all that God wants to pour in.

Now don't let the Adversary confuse you about the significance of water immersion or draw you into a commitment to religious rituals. All of our actions should symbolize something God is doing in us spiritually. For example, there is a spiritual significance in lying prostrate before God in prayer. It represents our humility as sinful people in the presence of a holy God. However, lying prostrate before God is not going to help us if there's pride in our hearts. Those prayers will be a stench in his nostrils.[122]

In Mark 7:1-23, Yeshua is questioned by the P'rushim (Pharisees) and Torah-teachers (teachers of the Law) about the ceremonial uncleanness of his disciples. He then quotes Isaiah 29:13 and says, "These people honor me with their lips, but their hearts are far away from me. Their worship of me is useless, because they teach man-made rules as if they were doctrines.'" In saying this, Messiah was admonishing the religious leaders for creating rituals and believing that they were pleasing to God. "Humans look at the outward appearance, but ADONAI looks at the heart."[123] Every religious act we do with our bodies should do one of two things: 1) represent something God has done in our hearts, or 2) submit our bodies to God so that He might do something in our hearts. If we participate in any religious act or do tzedakah (acts of righteousness) for a reason other than those two, our worship is useless.

Immersion in the Ruach HaKodesh (Holy Spirit)

God desires to rule every aspect of our lives. So, He has given us a way to be personally connected to Him at any given moment: it's His Ruach HaKodesh. The Ruach HaKodesh was sent to us by the Messiah,[124] just after He was taken up into glory.[125] The Ruach HaKodesh serves many functions: He teaches us,[126] He tells us the will of the Father,[127] He brings Yeshua's words back to our remembrance,[128] He cleanses us,[129] He guides us,[130] He empowers us to work for God,[131] He prays for us and with us,[132] and He testifies to the world that we are children of God.[133] Immersion in the Ruach HaKodesh is an essential part of our transformation. The Ruach HaKodesh is an important part of the person of God. Just as we cannot see the Father except through the Messiah,[134] we need the Ruach HaKodesh for the world to see Yeshua in us. John 20:21-22 reads, "'Shalom aleikham (Peace be upon you all)!' Yeshua repeated. 'Just as the Father sent me, I myself am also sending you.' Having said this, he breathed on them and said to them, 'Receive the Ruach HaKodesh!'"

Water immersion, and the preparation for it, removes barriers and hindrances in our relationship with Yeshua. Through the process of water immersion, we are emptied of our will, desires and motives. Immersion in the Ruach HaKodesh refills us with the will, desires and motives of God for us in our next level. Thus, immersion in the Ruach HaKodesh gives us the power to represent the Messiah in our next level. The power that Yeshua promised to us is only possible when we receive the Ruach HaKodesh.[135]

We receive the Ruach (Spirit) at the time that we accept Yeshua as Adonai. However, we need more of the Ruach for every new level. Yeshua is a perfect example of this. We know that He already had the Spirit of the Holy God in Him throughout His entire life, because He is fully man and fully God. However, just after His water immersion, the Ruach descended upon Him like a dove.[136] This was the power of the Ruach that He would need to fast for 40 days while being tempted by Satan[137] and then begin His earthly ministry. The level of Ruach anointing that we receive is proportionate to our preparation and the level to which God is taking us in Him.

The Bible recounts Sha'ul's own immersion in the Ruach HaKodesh in verse 17 of Acts chapter 9. Sha'ul received the Ruach HaKodesh through the laying on of Hananyah's (Ananias') hands. Upon receiving the Ruach, the scales fell from Sha'ul's eyes. His perspective on life was immediately changed because of this immersion. Many believers receive the Ruach HaKodesh by the laying on of hands, as God often desires that the Ruach HaKodesh be transferred from one believer to another. The great thing about this is that the first believer doesn't lose the Spirit but is strengthened through her obedience. Kefa (Peter) and Yochanan (John), as did all of the emissaries (apostles), often laid hands on believers so that they might receive the Ruach HaKodesh.[138]

After being transformed by the renewing of his mind, Sha'ul began to proclaim the Word of God boldly (see verse 20). Sha'ul knew the Scriptures forwards and backwards through his training as a Parush (Pharisee). He was also well acquainted with the Good News of Yeshua the Messiah because of his dedication to persecuting believers. His sinful nature had perverted the Word of God though. Everything he knew and learned was colored by his sins. Yeshua purged him of his sins, however, leaving only the knowledge of the truth. After being immersed in the Ruach HaKodesh, he received the power and inclination to proclaim the Word of truth to the world. Similarly, when we receive a new anointing for the next level, things we have already learned and experienced become clearer. We are then able to deliver the same messages, minister to the same people and function in the same gifts with more power, authority and clarity.

We must continue to feed the Ruach HaKodesh in us with the Word of God, though, and receive the Word of God with the Ruach HaKodesh. One without the other will lead us to depart from God and misrepresent Him to the world. Later on in the book of Acts, Sha'ul meets a Jewish man named Apollos who spoke with fervor about Yeshua but only knew of Yochanan's immersion (water immersion). The believers took him with them to explain the way of God to him more adequately, because though he was well-learned, he needed more teaching and understanding through the Ruach HaKodesh.[139] When we go to another level, we, like Apollos, will need more training. God will put believers in our path who can help us continue to grow in Him. We must be open-minded and discerning in spirit, though, because they may fellowship outside of the circles and demographic groups we're used to. Don't limit God. The next level doesn't look anything like this one!

It's essential that our training in the Word be coupled with receiving the Ruach HaKodesh. No matter how much spiritual training we get, we will never fully understand the Word of a God who is spirit, unless we receive His Spirit. Luke 24:13-49 recounts Yeshua's interaction with two young men on another road. On this road to Amma'us (Emmaus), Yeshua explains the Scriptures to them. They were His disciples but hadn't understood the Word of God. It took an encounter with the resurrected Messiah for them to understand all that had been written about Him. The Father, Son and Ruach HaKodesh are one and the same.[140] If you receive the Ruach HaKodesh for your next level, you will be able to understand the Son, who is the Word of God,[141] in a next-level way. This new understanding will prepare you to go forward in obedience to all that the Father has called you to do in this new era of your life.[142]

Immersion in Fire

We may read the Word, we may understand what it means, but nothing can teach us to obey the Word of God like being immersed in fire. Obedience to God is not an innate characteristic that we have as believers; it must be learned. We learn to obey God's Word through making willing sacrifices, receiving discipline for our mistakes and being persecuted for the name of Yeshua. Sacrifice, discipline and persecution make up fire immersion, which is suffering. We suffer for cleansing, we suffer for our sins, and we suffer for the Messiah. When we persevere through it all, we come out stronger and more refined, in which case, fire immersion has served its purpose in our lives.

Fire immersion makes the words in the Bible come to life in our individual lives. We will never fully understand what "love your enemies" and "pray for those who persecute you,"[143] really means until we have been persecuted and taught through countless experiences that loving our enemies is the only way for us to be spiritually free during and after persecution. We learn how not to judge or condemn others through fire immersion. We learn to really trust God through the fire as well. Immersion in fire transforms us permanently into the men and women God created us to be by developing our character, changing our habits and revealing our true motives so that our minds might be transformed into the mind of the Messiah.[144] That's why immersion in fire is essential to our transformation into the likeness of Yeshua. Every time we experience preparation and cleansing (water immersion), then refilling and anointing (Ruach immersion), we can count on trials to come. This is our fire immersion.

Just after the Ruach descended onto Yeshua, He was led by the Ruach into the desert for 40 days to be tempted by the devil. This was His first voluntary fire immersion. Some of us are not so willing. Yet after walking with Yeshua for years, we come to realize that the fire will come just after the anointing, whether we want it to come or not. I hear God saying, "This can be easy, or it can be hard; you choose!" Though fire immersion is never without challenges, we make it much more difficult by refusing to accept that it is God's will for us, trying to escape the fire rather than walking confidently into it as Yeshua did, or giving up halfway through the fire immersion (which can be very painful and even fatal). Imagine a soldier deciding in the middle of a war that he doesn't want to fight anymore. Since the enemy is already present, the soldier would become easy prey. Just because we put down our weapons, doesn't mean Satan will put down his. He doesn't respond to requests for a "time out."

Let's look at Scripture to gain an understanding of God's purpose for the fire immersion of His people. Malachi 3:2-3 reveals to us that God refines His people like a refiner's fire for silver or gold. God often uses the analogy of refining silver[145] to help us understand that the way we're purged of sins is similar to the way silver is purged of impurities: by fire. The blood of Yeshua washes away our sins, but fire immersion changes our thinking and lifestyles so that we won't return to the sins from which we've been cleansed.

You'll notice that Malachi 3:2-3 specifically states that the sons of Levi are God's material for the refining. The Sons of Levi (Levites) are descended from Levi, a son of Ya'akov (Jacob)[146] (later named Isra'el[147]). Levi's descendants were given to Moshe's (Moses') brother Aharon (Aaron) as a tribe of priests.[148] They were set apart for the purpose of serving God. Though the sons of Levi were set apart, it was God's desire that the entire nation of Isra'el be priests to Him. Exodus 19:5-6 reads, "'Now if you will pay careful attention to what I say and keep my covenant, then you will be my own treasure from among all the peoples, for all the earth is mine; and you will be a kingdom of cohanim (priests) for me, a nation set apart.' These are the words you are to speak to the people of Isra'el.'"

This call to be priests was extended to Gentile believers as well through Yeshua the Messiah. Kefa (Peter) states, "you yourselves, as living stones, are being built into a spiritual house to be cohanim (priests) set apart for God to offer spiritual sacrifices acceptable to him through Yeshua the Messiah."[149] Later he adds, "But you are chosen people, the King's cohanim (priests), a holy nation, a people for God to possess! Why? In order for you to declare the praises of the One who called you out of darkness into his wonderful light. Once you were not a people, but now you are God's people; before you had not received mercy, but now you have received mercy."[150] In this, we see that Kefa (Peter) is not only speaking to his people Isra'el spread throughout the land but to the Gentile believers as well. Also, in Revelation chapter 5, the Lamb appears (who is the Messiah), and He is praised by all in heaven. Verses 9 and 10 read, "and they sang a new song, 'You are worthy to take the scroll and break its seals; because you were slaughtered; at the cost of blood you ransomed for God persons from every tribe, language, people and nation. You made them into a kingdom for God to rule, cohanim (priests) to serve him; and they will rule over the earth.'"

Beloved, we are the priests of God, whether Jew or Gentile. We're among those set apart for His service simply because we believe in His Son and submit ourselves to being transformed into His image. At the end of all things, the children of God will serve two purposes: to worship God in heaven[151] and to reign with the Messiah on earth.[152] Fire immersion prepares us to serve continually before the throne of God by purging us of our sinful ways, once and for all, and stripping away all that is unholy about us. Additionally, to be prepared for reigning with the Messiah on earth, we must be transformed into His likeness now, so that we might judge the earth in accordance with the Messiah as governors and rulers.

Every servant of God mentioned in the Bible was immersed in fire, refined to bring glory to the Father. Consider Iyov (Job), a man whom God called blameless and upright.[153] Iyov (Job), himself, stated, "Yet he knows the way I take; when he has tested me, I will come out like gold."[154] Though already blameless, Iyov (Job) was refined by God and thereby developed further and drawn closer to Him. Iyov (Job) is a wonderful example for us as to how we should go through the fire. I praise God that the book of Iyov (Job) is included in the Bible. God has used it to encourage me many-a-day while going through my own fire immersion.

Another servant in the Bible who was immersed in the fire was the emissary Sha'ul, our Biblical example of transformation. In verse 16 of Acts chapter 9, Yeshua foretells of his immersion. The Scripture reads, "For I myself will show him how much he will have to suffer on account of my name." Yeshua tells Hananyah (Ananias) that Sha'ul will certainly suffer throughout his life, and not because of his own sin, but because of the name of Yeshua. This suffering is his immersion in fire.

Sha'ul's life as an emissary was characterized by his fire immersion. It's chronicled in the book of Acts and throughout his letters to the communities of believers. He recounts his sufferings in 2 Corinthians 11:24-28 in which he states,

> "Five times I received 'forty lashes less one' from the Jews. Three times I was beaten with rods. Once I was stoned. Three times I was shipwrecked. I spent a night and a day in the open sea. In my many travels I have been exposed to danger from rivers, danger from robbers, danger from my own people, danger from Gentiles, danger in the city, danger in the desert, danger at sea, danger from false brothers. I have toiled and endured hardship, often not had enough sleep, been hungry and thirsty, frequently gone without food, been cold and naked. And besides these external matters, there is the daily pressure of my anxious concern for all the congregations."

He willingly suffered for the Messiah, and his reconciliation to God and transformation into a Messiah-like form was made complete.

Fire prepares the Bride

Present-day servants of God, like you and me, must also be immersed in the fire to fulfill the Bride's marriage vows to the Messiah, the Bridegroom. We can equate fire immersion to the trials and hardships all married couples endure. It's the hard times that bond a marriage and change the husband and wife into the people they should be for one another. Ask anyone who's been married over 20 years. It takes time to know someone so intimately that you meet their needs almost instinctively, you can make decisions for them without consulting them, and you can do what they would do in their absence. After being married that long, a husband and wife even start to look alike. God desires the same thing for the Body of Believers, that she would look and act, even think, like her Husband, who is Yeshua.

The sacrifice, discipline and persecution that make up fire immersion develop Messiah-like characteristics in us so that the Bride may resemble her Bridegroom. These characteristics were not taught in many of our home environments; they're not a part of our genetic makeup but come directly from God and are eternal. Trying to be like the Messiah from our own strength and understanding will always be short-lived. As soon as Satan sends someone to really try us, to do those things that we despise to the core of our beings, we'll revert back to our old characteristics.

Fire immersion teaches us over a period of time how not to respond as we used to, even when the unthinkable happens. We respond differently because a transformation has occurred in our thinking and in our souls, but this process takes time. It took years for us to pervert God's perfect work in us, and it'll take years for the corruption of our character to be undone. This is why believers say, "I'm a work in progress," or "Be patient; God's not done with me yet." Once fire immersion has created a Messiah-like characteristic in us though, no devil in hell can take it away. It becomes a part of us eternally because God's nature in us and the true people He created us to be are revealed, thus transforming the Bride into her God-ordained image.

Fire addresses our weaknesses

Despite the clear benefits of fire immersion, not many believers welcome this refining process into our lives. (I usually dread it.) Pain and suffering are not valued now-a-days as they once were. There was a time when people were put to the test through rites of passage and other coming of age experiences to train them for adulthood or some sort of service. Young people and those learning to serve, like in the military, were trained to stand up under pressure, to persevere when things got tough, and to value the experience for the building of their character. It's through challenges, physical, emotional and spiritual, that we grow and develop.

In today's society, we've learned to avoid such challenges though, developing only our strengths while we become weaker and weaker in our shortcomings. This makes Satan happier than a pig in slop because his job is to accuse the brethren.[155] Remember, Satan means accuser. He'll wait patiently for years, watching us build up our strengths and forget about our weaknesses, deluding ourselves into thinking that we've got it all together. Then, when we feel safe because we've surrounded ourselves with people and circumstances that don't challenge us, BAM, he attacks us in our areas of weakness, and we die in our sins as a result.[156] This is why successful millionaires jump off the roofs of their office buildings. A trap that was set years ago was finally sprung, and they weren't ready for it.

God doesn't desire that we be set up for Satan's trap. He wants us to address our weaknesses, our shortcomings, our secret sin areas, so that Satan can't use them against us. If we suffer from wrath, God will allow things to occur that continue to anger us, so that little by little we learn to control our tempers. If we suffer from unforgiveness, He'll send people into our lives who constantly screw up and hurt us until we learn how to forgive. Ya'akov (James) said it well. "Regard it all as joy, my brothers, when you face various kinds of temptations; for you know that the testing of your trust produces perseverance. But let perseverance do its complete work; so that you may be complete and whole, lacking in nothing."[157]

The fire immersion occurs throughout our walk as believers. It doesn't end until we are brought to God's goal for us.[158] Yeshua was well aware of the truth in that statement for Himself. In Luke 12:49-50, He says, "I have come to set fire to the earth! And how I wish it were already kindled! I have an immersion to undergo—how pressured I feel till it's over!" Additionally, Hebrews 2:10 states that the Messiah was brought to God's goal through suffering, and we know that we must follow His example. We're constantly being tried and changed. That's part of the purpose for our lives on earth.[159] When the fire immersion is complete and we're brought to God's goal for us, we'll be ready for service to God and taken up from this earth.[160]

Fire immersion on the altar

The Torah (Law of Moses) is filled with God's requirements for sacrifices, and those sacrifices were and still are an important part of worshipping Him. However, Yeshua was and is the final physical sacrifice for sins. His one-time sacrifice and victory over death has given us the authority to commune with God spiritually. Additionally, we, who live in fleshly dwellings,[161] are now made aware of forces in the spiritual realm and armed to fight those that are in rebellion to God.[162] Hence, we've now received a spiritual awareness not available before to beings in the flesh, namely humans.

Though we war in the spirit, ADONAI still requires sacrifices from His children. However, these sacrifices exist in the spiritual realm and affect occurrences in that realm, rather than in the natural. Hence, the flesh that we're to offer to God is our own sinful nature, rather than the flesh of animals. So, when I say, "we need to sacrifice flesh to God," I mean parts of our sinful nature, not actual parts of our physical bodies.[163]

God has never been satisfied with animal sacrifice, but rather with the motives behind the sacrifices. He has always wanted his people to sacrifice our flesh to Him. In Matthew 9:13, Yeshua says, "As for you, go and learn what this means: 'I want compassion rather than animal sacrifices.'" Sacrifices are also addressed in Hebrews chapter 10. Quoting Psalm 40:6-8, Hebrews 10:5-7 reads, "This is why, on coming into the world, he says, 'It has not been your will to have an animal sacrifice and a meal offering; rather, you have prepared for me a body. No, you have not been pleased with burnt offerings and sin offerings. Then I said, "Look! In the scroll of the book it is written about me. I have come to do your will."'"

Our flesh wants to be satisfied with an outward act to please God, but our spirits, once connected to the Messiah, know that a holy God requires holiness from His priests, which is who we are, and there is no other way to get into His presence.[164] Slaughtering an animal, even with its gore and required effort, is still significantly less challenging for us than putting OUR flesh on the altar before ADONAI. Only the Ruach HaKodesh can teach us as disciples of Yeshua to understand

and fulfill the Torah (Law). The emissary Sha'ul addresses this in 1 Corinthians 2:12-16 in which he states,

> "Now we have not received the spirit of the world but the Spirit of God, so that we might understand the things God has so freely given us. These are the things we are talking about when we avoid the manner of speaking that human wisdom would dictate and instead use a manner of speaking taught by the Spirit, by which we explain things of the Spirit to people who have the Spirit. Now the natural man does not receive the things from the Spirit of God—to him they are nonsense! Moreover, he is unable to grasp them, because they are evaluated through the Spirit. But the person who has the Spirit can evaluate everything, while no one is in a position to evaluate him. 'For who has known the mind of ADONAI? Who will counsel him?' But we have the mind of the Messiah!"

Yeshua didn't come to abolish the Torah (Law) or the Prophets, but to fulfill them.[165] With deliverance from captivity to sin He also brought a spiritual understanding of the Words and will of God. As we grow in the Body of the Messiah, the Ruach HaKodesh will continue to teach us how to understand and fulfill the Tanakh (Old Testament), every letter of it.[166]

So, let us allow the Ruach HaKodesh to teach us what it means to place our fleshly, sinful nature on ADONAI's altar to be immersed in fire. In Romans 12:1, Sha'ul writes, "I exhort you, therefore, brothers, in view of God's mercies, to offer yourselves as a sacrifice, living and set apart for God. This will please him; it is the logical 'Temple worship' for you." How then do we do this? Let's go to the Torah (Law). The beginning of Leviticus details the different sacrifices required by ADONAI. Chapter 1 addresses the burnt offerings made to God for sins. The "sinner" was to lay his hand on the head of the animal for sacrifice representing that the animal was taking his place as atonement for his sins. Then the animal was to be slaughtered, the blood splashed on the sides of the altar, the animal skinned and cut into pieces, the head and the fat arranged with the other body parts, the inner parts washed, and then all of that was thoroughly burned. The aroma was pleasing to ADONAI.

In chapter 2, we discussed our need for deliverance, being separated from the connections Satan has to us through our sin. We also discussed repentance in chapter 4; Messiah makes us aware of our sins, we acknowledge them, and, with His help, turn from them to God. Yet what do deliverance and repenting have to do with fire immersion? Well, God's requirements in the Torah (Law) for animal sacrifices show us the connection. The "sinner" presenting the animal had to place his hands on its head, also the place our sins begin, in our minds. Hence, our deliverance must begin in our minds as well, a new thought planted into our heads that what we're doing is a sin.[167] Then Adonai can convict our hearts, thus bringing us to a place of submission.

Here is where the altar comes in. In order to be transformed in an area of our lives, we must lay ourselves on God's altar to have Him burn up our flesh completely. Otherwise, we'll return to the same sins. The sin in us, which comes from our sinful nature, must then be totally slaughtered. Its blood, that which gives it life, must then be splashed on ADONAI's altar. The blood is self-will. We sin because it is our will to sin. Hence, we must surrender our will to God to receive His will for us. It must be skinned to show us what is covering it up; in effect, why were we kept from addressing it this long? We must cut it to pieces, or thoroughly dissect it, by allowing the Ruach HaKodesh to show us the different forms that sin takes in our lives, why we like it, what keeps drawing us to it and what effects it has on us and those around us. The head must be cut off. This is the greater issue that drives the sin in us; the real reason we commit the sin; the strong man,[168] if you will. The fat must also be cut away. These are the things we've filled our lives with in order to make it easy for us to commit the sin. Our inner parts must be washed thoroughly because surely there was something impure in our hearts that allowed us to dwell on the thought of sin once it came to mind. Lastly, we must immerse it all in the fire, everything!

When God delivered me from fornication, I had to stay on the altar because I couldn't change on my own. I had to surrender my will to fornicate and receive God's will for celibacy. A rationalization that sex in monogamous relationships is okay was the skin that had to come off. When I cut fornication to pieces, I found lusting with my eyes, fantasies, sexually explicit movies, and romance novels, which all had to go. The head, the need for romantic intimacy, had to be burned up too. I learned that romantic intimacy is important, but dangerous outside of marriage. So, being married to Yeshua, I had to learn to look only to Him for intimate fulfillment. The fat of sexy lingerie, revealing clothes, and going to places where I might meet men were eliminated. My heart then had to be washed because of the deep desire I had for romantic intimacy at any cost to numb my pain. That was my logical Temple worship for that season of my life.

There are times when we haven't even committed a sin with our bodies but Yeshua points out sin in our hearts. During these times, we must present a burnt offering of birds, as described in Leviticus 1:14-17. Adonai showed me in a vision that the dove or young pigeon represents the heart. I saw a dove laid on a stone altar. Its wings were pulled so that its body ripped apart in the middle at the front. Then I saw a human heart float over the bird and rest on top of its body. I could still see the form of the dove through the heart though. I noticed that the body of the bird and the human heart were similar in size and shape, not a coincidence.

When a bird is sacrificed, the head is removed, just as with the offering from the herd or the flock. This shows us that there is still a deeper issue in sins of the heart that must be addressed. Blood is drained out on the side of the altar, which shows us that we still have a matter of self-will to address. Then the insides are removed, the New International Version says, "scooped out," and this is what we must allow God to do, scoop out the impurities in our hearts. These are the desires, plans and emotions that displease Him. The feathers from its neck were plucked out representing our haughtiness in believing we can conceal the contents of our hearts from God and persist in plans that displease him. All of these must then be immersed in the fire.

I recently had to make a burnt offering of birds to ADONAI. I haven't committed an act of fornication in many years. Yet Yeshua showed me that there still was some impurity in my heart that was not removed during the sacrifice that I made to be cleansed of fornication. In my testimony, I shared that Yeshua has been a Husband to me. Yet, even after Yeshua began ministering to my soul and God blessed me with my husband, there was still an obsession that could pull my life out of order. The Messiah showed me that the desire for intimacy to address pain in my soul still rested in my heart. In my marriage, I have sacrificed time with God, fulfilling His will for me, serving in my home and even ministering to my children to feed this deep-seeded need for romantic intimacy.

I was a daddy's girl as a child. My dad first left home when I was about seven years old. From that point on, my parents' relationship was off and on, so a need for the consistent security and comfort of a man was lacking in my life. It was this need that created my desire for romantic intimacy to address my pain. Because my desire was attached to an old emotional deficiency, it became very unhealthy and almost obsessive. Yet after I began walking with Messiah, my sin in this area was more subtle, thus hidden from me, due to my knowledge of the Word of God and sincere love for Him. But I praise ADONAI that He is a revealer of mysteries.[169]

God showed me that this desire for emotional intimacy had caused me to act and react out of emotion rather than obedience to Him in my personal life. Now that I'm aware of this and have made my sacrifice unto the Lord, I'm able to check my motives when I make decisions, ask for His strength when I know a test is coming up and choose the harder road of being alone whenever it fits into God's will for me at the time. I'm more obedient, I value my time alone with God and myself more, and I minister more effectively to everyone in my life, including my husband, because I'm not looking as much to have my needs met, but rather to meet the needs of others.

My initial burnt offering for deliverance from fornication did exactly what it was meant to do. However, once God removes one level of sin from our souls, He reveals a deeper need beneath the surface. Hence, it's important that we continue to allow God to immerse us in the fire for cleansing throughout our lives. Receiving the revelation that a burnt offering of birds needs to be made is a lot harder than receiving the revelation about the need for a burnt offering from the herd or flock. Those offerings have a physical sin attached to them that's easier to receive conviction for than a deep desire, plan or emotion that hasn't yet manifested itself as blatant sin. There is still sin present, however, when a burnt offering for birds is needed. It's just more subtle, yet more deadly because it can be used against us by the enemy later in life, when we feel secure. Only the risen Savior can reveal it, and then only if we really desire to be pure and holy, in every area.

Now you may ask, "Exactly where am I supposed to present this sacrifice to ADONAI; where is my altar?" Let's take a lesson from our common father in the faith, Avraham (Abraham). Avraham and his son Yitz'chak (Isaac) built altars wherever they had encounters with God.[170] We should do likewise. Whenever we have an encounter with God, a God-sighting as I call them, we can present ourselves on the altar as a sacrifice, living and set apart. Our prayer closets are our altars, and they can be anywhere we are. As long as we can spend some uninterrupted time with the Messiah, we can "build an altar" and lay our flesh on it.

These God-sightings might not only occur to convict us of sin. We also need to present a burnt offering when God makes a new promise to us or reveals Himself to us in a new way. Consider this, the words "altar" and "alter" are pronounced the same way; this is not a coincidence for God invented languages.[171] Hence, every time we need to be altered (transformed) we need to go to the altar and present some flesh for immersion in fire.

As you'll recall, we discussed the need in our flesh to use outward actions to replace true worship of God. Every act not done as a result of our faith in Him is sin.[172] This is important to remember because we can't just create a recipe for deliverance or a rule book for being set free and think that this will please ADONAI. Nothing can replace true fellowship of

God and hearing from Him yourself. Each fire immersion you experience may be different, so don't get locked into doing things a certain way, or try to follow my examples above "step by step" to get your deliverance. That's not how God works. This book (and other reference materials He's sending to you) is just a guide to plant seeds in your heart and mind that the Word of God and the Ruach HaKodesh will have to water. Don't allow ritualism to slip into your deliverance. Listen for God's voice, and He'll tell you the specific things you must do and when you must do them to receive a greater level of purification and anointing.

Discipline as fire

Sacrifice is offering ourselves willingly that we might suffer for the sake of the Kingdom. Discipline, however, is suffering planned by ADONAI as a consequence of our sins. Discipline is an important part of our transformation from sinner to servant, but it's also painful. How can we, as believers, readily accept God's discipline when we don't even see the value in disciplining our own children anymore? I admit, I struggle a lot with disciplining my children because it causes me pain. Yet Yeshua reminded me that Proverbs 23:13-14 clearly states, "Don't withhold discipline from a child—if you beat him with a stick, he won't die! If you beat him with a stick, you will save him from Sh'ol (death)."[173]

Like most of us, I feel that if I'm too harsh, I'll hurt their feelings or scar them emotionally, so I sometimes let things go unpunished, to their detriment. However, God, the perfect parent, disciplines us. In fact, I can't speak for you, but I've received many whippings from God. How I discipline my children is nothing compared to how God disciplines me. That's because discipline is an act of love. God loves perfectly, so He disciplines perfectly (and completely, believe me).

Hebrews chapter 12 tells believers to "regard your endurance as discipline" because it shows that we're true children of God.[174] It even likens God's discipline to the discipline we received from our natural fathers.[175] However, we can't understand this analogy if we're unable to see purpose in the discipline we received from our parents. If that describes you, it could be due to your own lack of understanding (which God can fix if you ask) or it could be due to your parents' under or over disciplining, both of which lose their effect. Furthermore, some believers have no point of reference on this topic, because they didn't receive any discipline at all. No matter what the case is for you, know that God is a perfect Father. He never wants to harm us, but He doesn't want anyone else to be able to harm us either. Hence, discipline teaches us to fight the Adversary.

Our views of our earthly parents are transferred onto God until He can renew our minds. Hence, our view of suffering, specifically as caused by discipline, will significantly affect how we go through the fire. Once we can recognize the benefits of discipline, we'll thank God for it and continue to persevere through it. The Scripture in Hebrews continues, "Now all discipline, while it is happening, does indeed seem painful, not enjoyable; but for those who have been trained by it, it later produces its peaceful fruit, which is righteousness."[176]

I must add that it's not a coincidence that the chapter on discipline in Hebrews comes directly after the chapter on faith. God is perfect in all He does. During our times of trial, we must trust that He is in control and allowing things to happen to us for our own good.[177] Then we'll be able to say, as Hizkiyahu (Hezekiah) did, "The Word of ADONAI which you have just told me is good."[178] He didn't say the Lord's discipline was fair; he said it was "good" recognizing that it will come to an end that will bring glory to God and produce righteousness in His people.

Persecution as fire

Discipline is not the only suffering outside of our control that we undergo in the fire immersion; there's also persecution. The difference is that discipline is justified punishment for our shortcomings. Persecution is suffering for the Name of Yeshua, meaning we suffer because we ARE doing the will of God. This is why Yeshua says, "How blessed are those who are persecuted because they pursue righteousness! For the

Kingdom of Heaven is theirs. How blessed you are when people insult you and persecute you and tell all kinds of vicious lies about you because you follow me! Rejoice, be glad, because your reward in heaven is great—they persecuted the prophets before you in the same way."[179]

Believers don't enjoy suffering anymore than anybody else. However, as followers of the Messiah, we must rejoice in our sufferings and praise God through our pain. Persecution is a part of God's will for our lives. Sha'ul stated in 2 Timothy 3:12, "and indeed, all who want to live a godly life united with the Messiah Yeshua will be persecuted." In Matthew 16:23, Yeshua rebukes Satan who has incited Shim'on (Simon) to reject the way of suffering persecution. In the Scripture, Shim'on had just acknowledged Yeshua as the Messiah. Yeshua then renamed him "Kefa" ("Peter"). Then Yeshua tells them that He must suffer, and Kefa rebukes Yeshua by telling Him that it doesn't have to be that way. Yeshua knew that Kefa didn't fully understand God's will (for he had not yet received the Ruach HaKodesh[180]). For this reason, Satan was using him to try to tempt Yeshua to depart from God's ordained plan of suffering persecution.

Satan will also try to tempt you, even through those closest to you, not to choose the road of suffering for the Messiah. He'll try to offer you an alternative just as he did Yeshua in this example and in the desert.[181] Satan will always try to get us to believe that we can achieve God's purpose through a shortcut or an easier, less painful route. Remember Yeshua said, "Go in through the narrow gate; for the gate that leads to destruction is wide and the road broad, and many travel it; but it is a narrow gate and a hard road that leads to life, and only a few find it."[182]

After the Messiah's death and resurrection, Kefa (Peter) did learn the importance of suffering persecution. He likened it to refining as well. In 1 Peter 1:6-9, he describes the importance of suffering in proving our faith in God, thus guaranteeing the deliverance of our souls. The Scripture reads,

"Rejoice in this, even though for a little while you may have to experience grief in various trials. Even gold is tested for genuineness by fire. The purpose of these trials is so that your trust's genuineness, which is far more valuable than perishable gold, will be judged worthy of praise, glory and honor at the revealing of Yeshua the Messiah. Without having seen him, you love him. Without seeing him now, but trusting in him, you continue to be full of joy that is glorious beyond words. And you are receiving what your trust is aiming at, namely, your deliverance."

Another benefit of immersion in fire is that it turns us into spiritual warriors. Not all of our persecution will come from humans; our struggles with evil spirits are much more prevalent. In fact, most attacks that come through people around us are actually the result of a spiritual attack against us as with Yeshua and Kefa (Peter). In Ephesians 6:12, Sha'ul said, "For we are not struggling against human beings, but against the rulers, authorities and cosmic powers governing this darkness, against the spiritual forces of evil in the heavenly realm." He continues on to talk about putting on the full armor of God, which can only be received and used in the spiritual realm.

Submission to our fire immersion guarantees the victory against these evil forces though. This explains Satan's persistency in trying to convince believers (starting with the Messiah Himself) to run away from persecution or fight the battles in our own, human strength. In Romans 8:37-38, Sha'ul says that we are "super-conquerors" through the one who has loved us and not even demons can separate us from the love of God that is in the Messiah Yeshua our Lord. Coming through the fire makes us stronger and more resistant to spiritual attacks. It also builds up the Body of the Messiah because we can share our testimonies, which encourage others and teach them how to come through their own fire shining like pure gold.

God does bless us, and He gives us peace and joy in this life. That doesn't, however, negate the necessity of suffering for the Messiah. Yeshua's fire immersion led Him to take up the cross. He calls us to do the same.[183] You will recall that Yeshua reached God's goal through suffering, and this is the way also for us to become more like Him.[184] Though we say we are His talmidim (disciples), we often don't desire to go through the fire as He did. We will have no part in His glory if we don't share in His sufferings.[185]

CHAPTER 7
BORN AGAIN

"'Yes, indeed,' Yeshua answered him, 'I tell you that unless a person is born again from above, he cannot see the Kingdom of God.'"—John 3:3

I love the springtime. Everything is born anew. New flowers bloom, trees grow new fruits or blossoms, butterflies come out of their cocoons, birds return, there are weddings, graduations and plenty of births. I can even smell the newness in the air, that the earth has been replenished and mankind is given yet another opportunity to enjoy the blessings God placed on earth for us.[186] It's almost what I imagine the Garden of Eden to be like.

Every spring we get the opportunity to see the results of new birth from death. The winter season is an end for lots of things; many animals hibernate or migrate, and the leaves or blossoms of plants wither and die. Germs and pollutants are destroyed as well by the rain and snow. This allows many things, those thought to be bad and those thought to be good, to die so that what God desires to create in the new season will be able to start off fresh without being tainted or stifled by things old.

God plans the same for our spirits after every water, Ruach and fire immersion. On our current level, we've learned how to stand on our own two feet, how to survive in the world and how to provide for ourselves. But, an encounter with the Messiah calls us to surrender everything we know, everything we are and everything we depend on, thus killing our old selves and our old ways of life, again.[187] When the old things in us die, God is then free to birth new creations in us. As newness is birthed in us, we can move into a new level of our relationship with Him and a new anointing within the Body of the Messiah.

Our periods of immersion are like incubation periods. This is another aspect of the symbolism of water immersion. Babies are immersed in the womb. They are free floating, suspended in amniotic fluids and totally dependant on nourishment from their mothers. We too are suspended, weightless in an unfamiliar environment during our periods of immersion. The water immersion (for spiritual cleansing), the Ruach immersion (for refilling) and the fire immersion (for testing) all prepare and develop us for the next level. However, we aren't born into the new level until the immersion process is complete. Though we have already been born again of the Ruach,[188] we must keep developing and maturing in our spirits,[189] so each new level requires a new birth in us.

Our lifelong transformation makes our spiritual birthing process continual. Just as we were humbled before the Messiah to be born into the light, we are humbled over and over again in various areas of our lives that God might birth something new in us. This birthing process repeats itself in different seasons of our lives, and it's guaranteed to come around just as we're guaranteed that the springtime will come again. Adonai said to me, "you don't have to be perfect to produce perfect fruit for the Kingdom; you just have to be in my perfect will for that season of your life." This means that we must allow God to do in us what He desires to do, when and how He desires to do it, in order to be lined up with His will for us. It's not sin that keeps us from bearing fruit, because the Lord knows that we're prone to sin due to our flesh but, rather, it is not allowing Him to develop us and cleanse us of our sins in His timing that keeps us from bearing fruit.

Preparing for the Birth

When God desires for us to bear fruit for Him in an area of our lives, He'll start by breaking up the unplowed ground in that area.[190] That means that He'll stir up things that are lying dormant inside of us; things that we've not addressed in years and probably thought were gone. This part of the process we discussed in chapter 2: On a Road to Destruction. Breaking up unplowed ground is an uncomfortable and often painful experience for us because we're the ground. We must be poked and prodded for air to get into tight, old spots. We have to be dug into with sharp tools, over and over again. As believers, we often run away from this part of the process, preferring to pretend that we're delivered and transformed in that area rather than actually being delivered and transformed.

The next thing God must do is plant something new in our ground.[191] This is where the rebirth begins. He unearthed and stirred up all the mess within us that would keep us from bearing fruit, now He must plant the seed that needs watering. We discussed this in chapter 3: Detoured by Yeshua. The seed is a call, a vision, a ministry He wants to birth through us, an assignment to share the Good News with specific people, or a revelation of who He created us to be in an area of our lives. The revelation may be that God didn't make you to be walked over. He created you to be bold, and that's what He wants to see. He might give you a glimpse of yourself as a bold person or a Scripture about boldness; that's your seed. Just something to let you know that He's about to do a new thing; it's really going to happen this time, and He wants to do it in you. His appearance on your road to Damascus is to plant a new seed.

The third thing that must occur is that the seed must be watered. We do this when we make a U-turn, as described in chapter 4. Water always represents the Word of God, so get into the Scriptures. Feed your spirit as much of the Word of God that He sends your way, and really mediate on it that it might help the seed He's planted in you to grow. In order for that seed not to die, it must be saturated with the Word. The Word of God will increase your faith when times get hard. The Word will give you patience to know that God will do what He said He would do even if it takes years. The Word will develop wisdom in you so that you won't kill the seed He's planted in you. The Word of God will also bring you closer to the Creator who is the lifesource for you and anything He wants to birth in you.

Let's take this planting analogy and look at it with regard to the birth of a child. Before a baby can be conceived, the womb of the mother must be prepared to carry a child. Many things need to be in order for a woman's body to be able to carry a baby; one physical sign of this process is menstruation. This then is the plowing part of the process because the ground for the seed is being prepared and cleansed. Next, the egg finds its place in the mother's womb and the father's sperm finds the egg. Thus, a seed is planted. Then we know that God determines whether the seed will receive life and grow into a child, which we can equate to the watering of the seed.

There are still two other things that need to occur: growth and harvest. Growth occurs in our immersion stage, as discussed in chapter 6. In a plant, we know what growth looks like; the plant sprouts out of the ground and begins to increase in size and strength. In the birthing process of a child, we're looking at growth in the mother's womb. Remember, we're talking about preparing for the birth. So, as we think of our own spiritual condition, we're not looking at growth after God has birthed something in us. Instead, we're looking at the growth that must occur BEFORE He can birth something in us.

Similarly, the harvest for a plant is clear as the farmer comes and picks the fruit, sickles the grain or whatever he must do to reap profit from his labor. In the birth of a child, the harvest comes when the child is born into the world and his mother can reap the fruits of her labor by holding that perfect, small creature with whom God has blessed her. God reaps a harvest from us when we're born into that which He desired to birth in us: the ministry, the calling, the anointing, the role in our lives, or the change in our character. The harvest I'm speaking of here is just us being transformed into a new creature in this area, not yet being used by Him through this new area of birth (we'll discuss that in Part III).

Let me share with you an example of this birthing process in my life. For some time, God was focused on the fruit of my lips, that is, everything that comes out of my mouth. In Matthew 12:33-37, Yeshua says to the P'rushim (Pharisees),

> "If you make a tree good, its fruit will be good; and if you make a tree bad, its fruit will be bad; for a tree is known by its fruit. You snakes! How can you who are evil say anything good? For the mouth speaks what overflows from the heart. The good person brings forth good things from his store of good, and the evil person brings forth evil things from his store of evil. Moreover, I tell you this: on the Day of Judgment people will have to

give account for every careless word they have spoken; for by your own words you will be acquitted, and by your own words you will be condemned."

Additionally, Ya'akov (James) adds,

> "With it [the tongue] we bless ADONAI, the Father; and with it we curse people, who were made in the image of God. Out of the same mouth come blessing and cursing! Brothers, it isn't right for things to be this way. A spring doesn't send both fresh and bitter water from the same opening, does it? Can a fig tree yield olives, my brothers? or a grapevine, figs? Neither does salt water produce fresh."[192]

God desires for me to speak His words from my mouth, words that are life to His children and death to His enemies. The Scriptures above tell us that my heart must be pure in order for the Word of Truth to pass through my lips. Hence, God began breaking up fallow ground in my heart.

The plowing of my heart wasn't easy for me (and He will probably not be done until I die). At one point, it seemed as if every foul thing that had ever existed in my heart was being brought up. In those months, I saw pride, selfish ambition, fury, lust, envy, low self-worth, self-pity, people pleasing, and idolatry all surface in my heart. This particular plowing was harder for me than any other because God was ripping up so much in my heart at one time. He was bringing up the roots of other issues I've previously had. The surface sins had been removed, but apparently roots were still left there, otherwise they wouldn't have been coming up.

I praise God that He will never put more on me than I can bear, so I knew at the time that I would not only make it through the press, but also that the anointing waiting on the other side was going to be great. God wouldn't have plowed up this much ground in my heart if He wasn't planning to reap a mighty harvest. I know because I know the LORD my God; He doesn't waste His time.

God revealed to me my specific mission on earth: to prepare the way for Messiah's return. He shared with me the reason I'm here; this was a seed sown into my heart. He has placed various calls on my life, and He's shown me many things about myself, but this particular seed was different than the others. It actually included every other call, gift and anointing I've ever received. He connected them together for one mission. This seed also gave meaning to all of my past sins, my shortcomings and every bad experience I've ever had in my life. The seed revealed my purpose and thus added purpose to everything in and around me.

As I said earlier, the plowing season is purposeful. It's directly related to the harvest God wants to produce in us. So, remember what God showed you when we looked at our roads to destruction. The seed He plants in you will be in direct contrast to the thing from which Yeshua detoured you. Were it not for the seed He planted in me of my specific mission on earth, I wouldn't have been able to withstand the plowing I was going through. However, I know that in order for God to birth something new through me, He has to give birth to something new in me. The person I was during that plowing season couldn't possibly be used by God to birth a book about transformation to the Body of the Messiah, which includes Messianic Jews and Christians. But the person He gave birth to in me—with a new spiritual awareness, a new anointing, and the next level of faith—I can. I know because God said it, and I believe Him.

Being born again isn't easy. We have to fight for our lives every time, and each level of transformation is a new birth. We'll experience plowing, planting, watering, growth and harvesting (which is the birth) each time. Being born of the Ruach was just the beginning. Learning to live, fight and overcome in the Ruach transform us into the perfected creations God saw in us when He saved us in the first place. God has borne a wife, a mother, a student, a teacher, a lover of His Word, a worshipper, a minister, a prophet, an apostle, an entrepreneur, and an author in me. He's now giving birth to an innovator and global leader in me, and He's just getting warmed up. (Hallelujah!) He wants to birth just as much in you. The limit is set only by how much you will believe in Him.

Babes in the Messiah

After Adonai gives birth to a new thing in us, we become babes in that new area. It's funny, because as believers we're much like children in school. As soon as kids finally make it to the top of the heap in elementary school, they go to the bottom of the barrel in middle school. The process is the same for us. We have to be developed all over again each time God births something new in us.

I was a prophet before I was a wife (the second time, in God's ordained will). So, while I was somewhat mature with regard to prophesying, I was a newborn babe as a wife. Both the semi-mature prophet and the completely immature wife existed in the same believer. Needless to say, I was struggling, and still do sometimes. But I have learned that we can't forsake our development in one area to focus on another. It's also foolish to apply our spiritual maturity (because that's what we're talking about, not emotional or mental maturity) in one area of our lives to another area. Even being a mature leader in the Body like a rabbi or pastor, doesn't mean that you're a mature parent to your children at home. We can do all the things we need to do in the natural realm, and still not be spiritually mature in an area of our lives. Additionally, we can walk in a role for decades and still be spiritual babes in that area because our years of experience only count toward our spiritual development if we are lined up with God's Word and in His will for our lives during that time.

Pause for a moment to take an inventory of your spiritual maturity in every area of your life. Ask God to reveal all of the areas of your life to you such as marriage, ministry, relationship with Yeshua, family, finance, physical health, etc., because you may overlook an area or receive revelation that an area has been left untended for years. Then sit before God and inquire of Him about your spiritual maturity in those areas. He knows what you were created to be and what you need to do to be transformed into that creation. He does not evaluate us based upon our actions nor does He measure us against each other; instead, He looks at our hearts[193] and measures us against the finished works of Yeshua within each of us.[194] Listen carefully to what God is saying to you now about your spiritual maturity in every area of your life so that you will really receive this Word, because it is for you.

Let's look back at our Biblical example of Sha'ul, for his transformation vividly depicts a rebirth. Not only did the Messiah detour him on his road to destruction, but He also changed Sha'ul from a persecutor of the brethren into a believer in Yeshua as the Son of God. All of this occurred in one moment of appearing before him on the road to Damascus. Verses 8 and 9 of Acts chapter 9 show us that Sha'ul's experience with the Messiah was so powerful that he lost his sight. He had to depend totally on those around him, because he was left helpless, like a baby. Sha'ul's physical blindness gives a great example for us of our condition directly after a birthing process in our spiritual lives: we're totally helpless.

The Messiah calls us to repent, to turn away from our sins to God, but how do we turn to God in that area of our lives? If we knew the answer, we would've already been headed in that direction. Because we now have a new outlook and are taking on a new way of life, we become just like babies. We have to be taught and nurtured all over again. The difference, however, is that this birth is a spiritual birth, in that our physical bodies still function as they did before, but we have no idea how to use our spirits in this new area.

Our spirits function differently than our bodies. They do need nourishment, but spiritual food is the Word of God.[195] Once again, we see the importance of the Scriptures in our lives. This theme will keep coming up, so make your peace now with studying the Word daily. Additionally, our spirits need to be connected to the life-giving God, through the Ruach HaKodesh, to grow in strength.[196] The Counselor (Ruach),[197] given to us by the Messiah, is our direct link to God. He sends us every message we need to receive and teaches us everything we need to know so that we can continue to be fed by the Father.

When a baby is born, he has desires to do things such as run and talk. We can tell by the sounds he makes and the way he moves. However, he hasn't yet learned how to get his body parts to function, and he hasn't yet developed his thinking and his muscles to respond to commands from his will. The same is true for us after being born again in any area of our lives. We desire to please God, we desire to serve His people, and we desire to be more like the Messiah, but we have no idea how to do it.[198] The rebirth in our lives transforms us into a new creation; it doesn't, however, train us to live as this new creature.

I'll give you two examples of this in Sha'ul and myself. When Sha'ul was transformed from a Parush (Pharisee) bent on destroying believers to a believer on a mission, he didn't automatically know how to live as a believer. P'rushim (Pharisees) and believers in Yeshua lived very different lives in those days. His heart had been changed, but he had to make a conscious effort to allow God to change his attitudes, behaviors and lifestyle. This is why he stayed with the believers in Damascus for a while, then presented himself to the believers in Yerushalayim (Jerusalem); he was being trained to live as a believer and had to position himself for the training.

Similarly, when God began the process of birthing a prophet in me, He began to do new things in our relationship. As I shared with you, He has always spoken to me, but it was usually about me or someone close to me. During my rebirth, He began speaking about the global Body of the Messiah and local churches, the United States and the nation of Isra'el, end times and wars. Needless to say, I was terrified, but I also realized that something new was happening. Once I accepted His call to prophesy and took my vows before Him (just He and I), the prophet in me was born. But the real work lay ahead. I then had to learn to BE a prophet. It's much more than hearing the voice of God and writing down or speaking what He says. God continually develops and trains me in this and all areas of His service, because maturity is a necessity.

After we experience a rebirth in the Messiah, we have to allow Him to develop our minds just as the minds of babies must be developed. There is a direct connection between the way we think and our obedience, or disobedience, to the Word of God. Sins begin as desires from our flesh, which are nurtured by our thinking, then give birth to action.[199] Obedience begins with a desire inspired by the Spirit of God. This desire, which comes through the seed planted during our encounter with the Messiah, must then be fed by godly knowledge to give birth to godliness.[200] Since we developed our minds in the flesh, we have to renew them in the Ruach.[201] We have to read God's Word[202], be taught by men and women of God[203] and pray for wisdom,[204] so that we can learn how to live our new lives.

He Sends Believers to Care for Us

We can't reshape our thinking alone because everything we take in, everything we read and hear, will be challenged by our old way of thinking. This happens almost automatically without us even noticing. For this very reason, God sends people to us who've had their minds renewed in similar ways, people who've been down the road we're traveling. The people God sends to us, in most cases, have had to dispel the same thoughts with which we're currently wrestling.

For example, God may send a woman whom He has delivered from a victim mentality to minister to a battered wife. This is necessary because the battered wife may suffer from low self-esteem and a lack of trust. Every Word she receives about God's love for her or His desire for her to have faith in Him would be rejected because her suffering has altered her thinking. She wouldn't even understand why she was rejecting God's Word, but her personal relationship with Yeshua would suffer, and she would never develop the faith she needs to lean on Adonai. The woman God sends, who herself was delivered from a victim mentality, can minister to the battered wife about the sincere and deep love of God and counsel her to recognize, honestly address, and surrender to God her feelings of insecurity and mistrust. Though these feelings are understandable considering her past experiences, they come from trusting in sinful man and cannot be applied to the holy God in His perfect faithfulness.

Our upbringing and experiences in life help to create our worldviews and develop defense mechanisms in us. In order for us to hear the voice of God clearly, and accept His Word as truth, we must allow God to change our thinking. We have constructed our lives around our thinking, so this is not an easy process. Our personal priorities, our values, even our identities are built upon the foundation of our thinking. None of us would readily surrender our priorities, values and identities without the realization that they've been built upon flawed and unstable foundations.[205] Other believers can help us to recognize the flaws in our thinking through fellowship, counseling, teaching and proclaiming to us the Word of God. They can also encourage us to be devoted to prayer and Bible study, especially when times get rough in our lives and we're tempted to forsake the way of the cross.[206]

When I say, "other believers," I don't mean the ones with whom we always fellowship. If God is doing a new thing in us and taking us to a new level, we will need to fellowship with new people, people who are already on that new level. This is essential to our development, because they will challenge our thinking. I'm not suggesting that we change congregations or denominations when God desires to develop us, but we must broaden our fellowship circles. If the people with whom we regularly fellowship had all that we need to develop into our next level, we would already be there. As God desires to expand our thinking, we must open our hearts to expand our relationships. Please note that the new people ADONAI sends to us may be mature on our new level but immature on our levels of maturity. This shouldn't be a deterrent though. Instead, it's a sign that we're on the right path. God is an investor; while He's using someone to develop something in you, you can be sure He's using you to develop something in them.

God cares for Sha'ul in verses 10 through 19 in Acts chapter 9, knowing that he was just born into the light.[207] The disciple Hananyah (Ananias) had the task of being used by God to restore Sha'ul's sight. Sha'ul's blindness is an example for us about changing our perspectives. The way Sha'ul viewed the world was challenged by his encounter with the Messiah on the road to Damascus. In the physical and spiritual sense, he was blinded by the Light. God ministered to his spirit during his days of fasting and prayer. Then He restored Sha'ul's vision through another believer. In essence, God used someone else to help him see the world a new way.

Hananyah (Ananias) was blessed as well. Being called to go to Sha'ul challenged him to release judgment to God and made him take on a new level of faith. In verses 13 and 14 of Acts chapter 9, he objects to being sent to Sha'ul. He may have been afraid of Sha'ul because he had been imprisoning believers and voting for them to be killed. He may have been angry with Sha'ul because he had been an enemy to believers everywhere. Either way, being sent to Sha'ul was a challenge. We see that God's transformation in Hananyah (Ananias) was complete as well though. In verse 17 when he appears to Sha'ul, he addresses him as "Brother Sha'ul," boldly leaping out into the uncharted waters of the next level of faith God had given him. At this point, no one had testified to him about Sha'ul, no one except Yeshua. And Hananyah (Ananias) ministered to Sha'ul in love. Had Sha'ul rejected Hananyah's ministry, they both would've missed out on a blessing of transformation.

When Sha'ul's vision was restored, he saw the world differently. He didn't return to his old perspective but viewed the world through his new spiritual eyes given by God. This is what the elders mean when they ask God to remove the scales from someone's eyes. They're praying that Adonai will change the person's perspective, so that they will no longer see the world or their current situation as they desire to see it or as the world has taught them to see it. Instead they'll see things as God sees them, with spiritual eyes.[208]

Hananyah (Ananias) had the anointing to help Sha'ul see things differently because he was a Messianic Jew himself with spiritual revelation. A Parush (Pharisee) could not have been used to restore Sha'ul's sight because he would be just as blind, spiritually, as Sha'ul. Yeshua was birthing a Messianic Jew with spiritual revelation in Sha'ul, so that's who

He used in his healing. We must be open to the new places to which God will take us and the new people God will place around us during the first stages of our new birth onto the next level. These people and places have the anointing we need to develop our next-level maturity. We must see them as gifts and not fear the change.

Viewing Life with Spiritual Eyes

Just as our thinking developed based upon our desires and our flesh, so has our vision. We recognize things going on in the natural world around us yet fail to recognize all that occurs in the spiritual world around us.[209] When we are born again of the Ruach, we're given a greater ability to discern what occurs in the spiritual realm as well. Many of us believe in the existence of angels, or good spirits, yet most of us to don't believe in the existence of demons, or evil spirits. If God is spirit and we must worship Him in spirit and in truth,[210] doesn't that tell us that we must begin not only to see into but also function in the spiritual realm? We're being transformed into the likeness of His Son, who was feared by demons when He walked the earth.[211]

Every time we're born again of the Ruach, we get the chance to move up a level in the fight to reclaim the earth and everything in it exclusively for God and His people. The battle begins first on our own home turf. No, I'm not talking about fighting for our families or our homes, though we must fight for them continually. But it begins even closer than that—in our own minds. Before being detoured on a road to destruction, our thoughts are even displeasing to God, and those thoughts lead us to depart from Him. In order to have a renewed mind, we must begin to think like Yeshua in the area of our new birth. As our spirits develop, we increase our ability to do just that, which affects every aspect of our lives.[212]

Each time we are born again of the Ruach, we receive another level of anointing from the Ruach, which is a part of the person of God. Thus, we receive another aspect of God into our very being. The Ruach works to renew our minds in a new area, because some things we value are sinful to God and some things we think are foolish actually display faith in God.[213] We're unable to understand these things until the Ruach reveals them, because the flesh sees the world with natural eyes, only acknowledging the information directly in view or recollected from past experiences.[214] Once our minds are renewed, we're able to view the world, in the area of our new birth, through the eyes of God. This point of view is based upon faith in God's sovereignty, holiness and love. We then are capable of making truly wise decisions in that area, just as the Messiah did during His ministry here on earth, for we have received the same Ruach that empowered Him though He lived in an earthly vessel.

It doesn't matter how wise a person is, making judgments based on data from only the past and present will always leave much room for error. There will inevitably be things we can neither account for nor predict in the future. God, however, sees and knows everything. Not just the past and present, not just the people involved in the situation, but He also knows the future and everyone who will be inadvertently affected. Once we understand this, we realize that there's no wiser choice than to submit to God and allow Him to renew our thinking and change our point of view after each new birth.

Chapter 8
Saved, Sanctified and Holy Ghost Filled
-Regina's Testimony-

"But now I am going to woo her—I will bring her out of the desert and I will speak to her heart. I will give her her vineyards from there and the Akhor[215] Valley as a gateway to hope. She will respond there as she did when young, as she did when she came up from Egypt."
—Hosea 2:14-15

    Regina grew up in the church and knew the Word of God, but there was a time in her life when living by the Word wasn't so easy to do. As a young woman, Regina fell in love with a man she believed in her heart that she would marry. Being raised in the church, she just knew that they would be married because they were close, they had been together for a long time, and he was the first and only man she had loved with her heart and her body. He was unfaithful to her though and got Regina and another woman pregnant around the same time. To Regina's devastation, he married the other woman.

    Needless to say, Regina found herself heartbroken, alone and left to raise their only child as a single mother. The shame of having a child out of wedlock wasn't the tough part for her, nor was having to work two and three jobs to take care of her child but having to see the consequences of her choice on her child made her feel helpless. She stood watching as her daughter waited by the window from morning to night for daddy to show up, and he never came. She felt guilty for having a child with a man who was neither responsible for the child nor present in her life. She worried about how her daughter would be affected in the long run by her absent father. So, as any mother would, she worked hard to make sure that her daughter had a relationship with her dad. Yet all the while, she still held strong feelings for this man.

Out of loneliness and her love for him, they began to have an affair. He would come into town to visit his family members and spend time with his daughter, and it always led to them being together. She then found herself not only committing fornication, but also adultery, because he was still married to someone else.[216]

No matter how she tried, she couldn't justify this relationship in her mind. She knew that having a child with him wasn't an excuse, nor was him being her first love; he wasn't her husband, and though she longed for him, they shouldn't be together. Her desire for him to have a relationship with their child made it even harder for her to break off their affair because she knew he expected to see her every time he came to see their daughter. As a mother, she desired for them to have a close relationship, but she needed to break free from him herself.

Throughout this period in her life, she continued to go to church and worship God. However, she was convicted every Sunday about her relationship with him, but she felt powerless to make a change. Week after week she would flood the altar with tears, but then she would return to spending time with someone else's husband. She knew something had to be done, because she was making herself available for this man whenever she knew he was in town. Yet all the while, she was building up resentment about being the other woman, because in her heart she knew that she would never be his wife. The truth of the matter was that she desired to have her own husband, she wanted to be pleasing in God's sight, and she was tired of allowing her daughter to watch her continue in this affair.

Finally, God began to move in her life through a women's fellowship at her church. Regina joined the women's fellowship and began to talk about her situation. Women there ministered to her so that she might be delivered from her bondage in this affair. At one particular service, God showed up in a mighty way. A prophet came to the church and spoke the Word of God to specific people in the congregation. During this service, the woman singled out Regina, and it seemed as if she looked right into her soul. Then she said, "God is going to return everything that has been stolen from you double-fold, but you have to let something go." Regina's spirit knew this was the Word of God, and she immediately fell out.

After this experience, she knew that she had to sever the relationship with the father of her child once and for all. The Ruach HaKodesh in her rose up with the unction to tell him that they could no longer see each other. She, however, still desired to be intimate with him. So, she planned one last night with him to tell him it was over but be intimate with him once more. At this point, her daughter was no longer living in the house and there was no reason for him to visit her. However, he still came by when he was in town.

On this particular evening, she told him that he needed to go home to be with his family and she asked for his forgiveness for making it easy for him to be with her though he was married. Even after saying all of that, she still desired to sleep with him once more, but God sent him out of the door. The speech the Ruach had given him through her made him so uncomfortable that he had to leave, thus giving her a way to escape out of the plan she made to sin again.

Regina's transformation didn't happen overnight. There were some things she had to do. She made sure she was not at home when her daughter's father was in town. Instead, she would be at church or in fellowship with women of the church. She had to feed her mind with the Word of God to keep her spirit strong. She had to stay in fellowship with believers and continue to deal with her feelings toward this man and the spiritual ties that she had to him. Sure, she was tempted to fall into fornication again, but the Ruach HaKodesh would always show up by making her visualize God watching her while she's sinning or by making the man feel uncomfortable because of the clear anointing on her life.

God sent some spiritual mothers to Regina during this time in her life, because He knew that she needed help to get through this. She had loved the father of her only child for almost 20 years. What was she supposed to do now? Through the relationship with these women of God, she was able to talk about her feelings and also learn how to deal with everything going on in her heart and her spirit.

The women God placed in her life also began to notice spiritual gifts in her and acknowledge her call to minister. Regina started attending intercessory prayer sessions, but she prayed silently moving her lips. A minister at the church then told her to speak up during the prayer and when she did a wellspring of unknown tongues[217] erupted and flooded out of her. She couldn't stop herself from speaking, though she didn't know what she was saying. She was so overwhelmed by the gift that it knocked her out. Other gifts came soon after like discernment of spirits[218] and laying on of hands,[219] but she still needed to be taught how to use them. Her fellowship in the church allowed God to prepare her to be the woman He created her to be.

Today Regina is an ordained minister, elder, prayer warrior and wife. God uses her tremendously in the work of ministry and has placed on her life many calls and in her spirit many gifts. He positions her strategically so that He can use her for His own purposes, while He continually trains her to be a godly wife to her husband. Her life isn't easy; I know because I have warred against the enemy alongside her, but through it all, God is faithful to always show up on her behalf, at home and at church, on time.

PART III
USED BY GOD

"In a large house there are dishes and pots not only of gold and silver, but also of wood and clay. That is, some are meant for honorable use and some for dishonorable. If a person keeps himself free of defilement by the latter, he will be a vessel set aside for honorable use by the master of the house and ready for every kind of good work."

2 Timothy 2:20-21

Chapter 9
Sharing the Good News

"I don't ask you to take them out of the world, but to protect them from the Evil One. They do not belong to the world, just as I do not belong to the world. Set them apart for holiness by means of the truth--your word is truth. Just as you sent me into the world, I have sent them into the world."—John 17:15-18

I was the commanding officer of the Marine Corps Junior ROTC unit in my high school. ROTC was one of my daily classes at school. Retired Marines taught us about conduct, leadership, values, marksmanship, and many other topics. It was such a meaningful experience that most of my classmates enlisted in the Marines right after our high school graduation. Every other year, we would take a trip to a Marine Corp training base to be trained like new recruits. People always say that basic training breaks you down to build you back up. I got a much better understanding of what that meant on one particular trip.

During my senior year, we went to a Marine Corps base called Parris Island. The drill sergeant and most of the other Marines there treated us like actual recruits. They even called us recruits. The pressure to immediately surrender my way of doing things and master a new way of doing them was more intense than I could've imagined. However, it was one of the most challenging, yet rewarding experiences of my life.

I recall fondly the land navigation course; they put us in the woods, gave us a compass and some directions and told us to get out before the snakes got us. Needless to say, I was the first one to finish that course. Chow time (mealtime) was my favorite part. We had to say in a bold voice what we wanted to eat for chow, or we got what they wanted us to have; I still don't know what that was. I learned real fast how to ask for chow. The hand-to-hand combat classes and obstacle course kicked my butt though, but I did learn how to crush someone's skull with the heel of my boot. (I praise God that I will never have to use that training, but God translated it into the spiritual realm in my call to be a soldier for the Messiah. I know how to crush the head of the enemy with my heel.[220])

At Parris Island, obedience and boldness weren't just good ideas, they were the keys to survival. But in order to learn these concepts, the person I was when I came there had to be immediately broken down, so that a Marine could immerge (or at least a Marine cadet). Now I would never imagine that my experience transformed me into a true Marine, but I really do have a sincere appreciation and respect for our fighting men and women after getting just a taste of what they willingly put themselves through daily for our country. Because I was a cadet, my military experience ended there, but for true Marines, bootcamp is just the beginning.

Like Marines, believers are broken down to be built back up. We have to be stripped in order to be built into mighty men and women of God who can not only make it to the next level but be victorious on that level. Hence, after all of the plowing, planting, growth and harvest, we have to actually DO something. Our preparation should serve a purpose: to produce fruit for the Kingdom of God. We've looked at Sha'ul's bootcamp experience as we've journeyed through this book together. He encountered Adonai on the road to Damascus, he fasted and prayed, he had visions about things God planned to do in his life, he was healed and immersed AND he was exhausted. He had spent three intense days with God, allowing himself to be completely broken and stripped bare. In verse 19 of Acts chapter 9, Sha'ul regained his strength after eating some food. He then spent several days with the believers in Damascus who helped to build him back up.

Transformation is a process of being broken down in order to be built back up, and it prepares us for the next level of work to which God has called us. There's a mission for each one of us related to God's perfect plan for the world. We're not capable of carrying it out as we are though. Through each transformation, God breaks us down to our weaknesses, those things we've spent a lifetime concealing, and then He builds us up to a higher level than before. This is all done so that we can represent Him well to the world.

We can expect this "breaking down to build up" process to repeat itself every time Adonai wants to do something new in our lives. If there's a new call, there will inevitably be a new bootcamp or transforming experience. The transformation, though important in itself, is only a means to an end, however. The real goal is for us to "go and make people from all nations into talmidim (disciples), immersing them into the reality of the Father, the Son and the Ruach HaKodesh, and teaching them to obey everything that I have commanded you."[221] The more we learn to obey, the more we can teach; the more immersions we undergo, the more of the reality of the Father, Son and Ruach we will know and demonstrate.

The Call to Proclaim the Good News

After having a personal encounter with the Messiah, or a God-sighting, we should want more than anything to share the experience with others. Being transformed is like receiving a wonderful new gift. Think for a moment about a child who gets the new toy she's wanted for months. She wants to show it to everyone and for everyone to play with it. Each time God shows up miraculously in our lives and transforms us in another way, we should share our testimony with others like the child with her new toy. We know that Sha'ul did this because in verse 20 he began to proclaim in the synagogues that Yeshua is the Son of God.

I praise God for the fire He puts inside of us after each transformation and revelation, because it's expected of every believer that we would go out and teach the world about the Messiah. This charge in Matthew 28:19-20 above, also known as the Great Commission, was not only for the men in the room with Him, but also for everyone who would come after them, including you and me. When the Messiah reveals Himself to us in a new way by delivering us from yet another level of sin and showing us how to defeat the Adversary in that area, we are obliged to share our new knowledge and experience with other believers so that they will be victorious in that area as well.

We can't limit this to just sharing the message of salvation; we must also share new insights God gives us into the spiritual realm, fresh and specific applications of Scripture and ways He renews our minds continually. The Great Commission doesn't read, "teaching them that I am the Deliverer." It reads, "teaching them to obey everything that I have commanded you." "Everything" means everything, not just the part about remission of sins. If God has taught you through Scripture how believers should minister to our families, then share that; the Body of the Messiah needs to know. And don't just share it within your fellowship group, ministry or denomination. All of us in the Body need to know what God has revealed to you. Write a book, publish an article or travel to various places (led by the Ruach) to teach and share your testimony. Think globally because we're all in this fight together. That's how we produce fruit 100-fold and get the most out of our struggles, pain and transformations.

Romans 10:13-15 stresses the importance of proclaiming the Good News, also known as evangelizing. It reads, "since 'everyone who calls on the name of ADONAI will be delivered.' But how can they call on someone if they haven't trusted in him? And how can they trust in someone if they haven't heard about him? And how can they hear about someone if no one is proclaiming him? And how can people proclaim him unless God sends them?—as the Tanakh (Old Testament) puts it, 'How beautiful are the feet of those announcing good news about good things!'" This Scripture, coupled with the Great Commission above, clearly relays the importance of sharing the Good News.

God desires that every person in the world be saved, so each of us must have the opportunity to choose Yeshua for ourselves and apply His teachings to our lives. We can't be saved from our sins if we don't understand how to apply the power of His sacrifice to all areas of temptation. It's our responsibility as the Messiah's friends,[222] brothers and sisters,[223] witnesses,[224] and joint-heirs to the Kingdom,[225] to introduce others to Him and deepen their understanding of how a risen Savior affects every aspect of their lives. Romans 10:15 asks, "And how can people proclaim him unless God sends them?" Through the Great Commission, the Messiah sends us, all of us, and each transforming experience we have with Him, points us in a specific direction.

Good News to Isra'el

Most Bible-believers have read Romans 10 as a call to evangelize, and we quote the Scripture above to help us understand the necessity of sharing the Good News of Yeshua. However, we rarely link the Old Testament Scripture referenced by Sha'ul (Isaiah 52:7) to this New Testament letter. Sha'ul is writing to a mostly Jewish congregation in Rome. Though there were many Gentiles as well, the Jewish majority in the body insured that the believers there were well acquainted with the Holy Scriptures (which at that time only consisted of the Old Testament). Hence, it was not necessary for him to quote all of Isaiah 52 in order for them to understand that he was referring to sharing the Good News with the children of Isra'el. Just mentioning the Scripture was enough to draw the members of the congregation to refer to Isaiah's prophecy concerning ADONAI's deliverance of the children of Isra'el.

Though Christians, for the most part, seem not to have put 2 and 2 together, all we need to do is read all of Romans chapters 9, 10 and 11 to understand Sha'ul's direction regarding a Gentile believer's call to share the Good News with the children of Isra'el. He goes on in chapter 10 to state that the Jews already heard the message and many rejected it, but God has used their disobedience to extend the invitation to Gentiles who are called to provoke them to jealousy.[226] Yet despite their rejection of the message, Sha'ul asserts in chapter 11, "all Isra'el will be saved" once the full number of Gentiles has come in.[227] This "fullness" refers to quantity—the nations must be well evangelized—as well as maturity—Gentile believers must reach maturity in faith, revelation and anointing to draw Isra'el back to the Jewish Messiah.

If we read Isaiah 52, starting at verse 7 and continuing to verse 10, we see that the prophet states that "all the ends of the earth will see the salvation of our God" when He comforts His people and redeems Yerushalayim. Is he referring to a physical deliverance such as described in Zechariah chapter 14 at the time of the Messiah's return? No! Isaiah 52 refers to the First Coming of the Messiah to claim spiritual victory for Isra'el and all the world through overcoming sin which leads to death. How do we know this? By continuing to read Isaiah 52 and 53; they are all about the Lamb of God.

In these chapters, the prophet depicts the Suffering Servant—the First Coming of the Messiah as the Lamb of God. This Lamb is exalted among all the nations and brings them to see what they have not even been told and understand what they have not even heard[228]—the salvation of God. The nations were not expecting a Messiah, so clearly Isaiah 53:1 does not refer to them. It reads, "Who believes our report? To whom is the arm of ADONAI revealed?" Sha'ul refers also to this text in Romans 10:16. Yet, both Sha'ul's letter to the Romans and the prophecy in Isaiah agree that Isra'el is spiritually redeemed by God through the Messiah's sacrifice.[229]

For proof of this, we must continue on in the book of Isaiah. Chapter 54 refers to Yerushalayim as God's bride[230] and states that though He has been angry with her, He will bring her back.[231] This is stated directly after describing the sacrifice of the Lamb led to slaughter in chapter 53. He will rebuild her and teach her sons[232] and no weapon forged against her will prosper,[233] after He has brought her back to Himself. As we know, reconciliation with the Father comes by only one means, through the Messiah.[234]

We must ask then, what role must Gentile believers play in the reconciliation of the children of Isra'el back to God through the Messiah? As a child of Isra'el himself, the emissary Sha'ul was perfectly qualified to teach us. He does so in Romans 9 and 10. In those chapters, he makes it clear that pre-believing Jews try to attain righteousness by works—obeying the law. However, our righteousness is based upon faith. It is this faith that receives God's mercy through the Messiah. We are then cleansed and made holy and not only empowered to obey the law, but to embody it just as Yeshua does. So, when Gentiles—who did not have the law, temple or patriarchs—represent the character and power of God, we provoke the children of Isra'el to jealousy. It is then made clear that righteousness comes by faith, not by works or even lineage.

Because God made the promise to Avraham, then Yitz'chak (Isaac) and later Ya'akov (Jacob), salvation has often mistakenly been connected to lineage. However, ADONAI says in Ezekiel chapter 18 that sons do not share in the guilt or righteousness of their fathers, but account for their own sins. Through the prophecy in Ezekiel, Adonai breaks down this mindset, so that each individual will realize that he or she must give an account to God. At the end of the chapter, He makes a plea to each child of Isra'el to repent and turn to Him. In like manner, Yeshua corrects the religious leaders who despised Him by telling them that having Avraham as their biological ancestor does not mean they are not enslaved to sin and in need of deliverance.[235] This is why we must share not only the message of salvation, but our testimonies of continual deliverance.

Thus, we see that it is a responsibility of Gentile believers to share the Good News of Yeshua with God's people Isra'el and demonstrate His love toward them. When we neglect this essential command of God, we fail to fulfill our purpose in the Kingdom.[236] And it is Good News to all. Being fully reconciled to God means we can all finally enter into His presence and even war in the spiritual realm, two blessings set aside for the children of God and current necessities for the children of Isra'el.

Satan desires to exterminate every Jew living on earth. After that, he wishes to kill all Gentile believers (and America is #1 on the hit list because of our Christian foundation). He has chosen this order because he understands God's order: salvation is to the Jew first, then the Gentile.[237] If you do not believe this, listen to the proclamations of the leaders of all of the enemy nations surrounding Isra'el. And if you are not sure why, consider the Scripture text below:

> "'In that case, I say, isn't it that they have stumbled with the result that they have permanently fallen away?' Heaven forbid! Quite the contrary, it is by means of their stumbling that the deliverance has come to the Gentiles,

in order to provoke them to jealousy. Moreover, if their stumbling is bringing riches to the world—that is, if Isra'el's being placed temporarily in a condition less favored than that of the Gentiles is bringing riches to the latter—how much greater riches will Isra'el in its fullness bring them. However, to those of you who are Gentiles I say this: since I myself am an emissary to the Gentiles, I make known the importance of my work in the hope that somehow I may provoke some of my own people to jealousy and save some of them! For if their casting Yeshua aside means reconciliation for the world, what will their accepting him mean? It will be life from the dead!"— Romans 11:11-15

The Adversary does not want God's people to know the truth because their collective acceptance of their Messiah means life from the dead for the whole world and the return of the Messiah to earth. In Matthew 23:39, Yeshua tells the Jewish religious leaders that they will not see Him there again (in the temple in Yerushalayim) until they cry out "Baruch haba b'shem Adonai" (Blessed is he who comes in the name of the Lord). This is why the full number of Gentiles must come in first. Otherwise we would not be ready for the magnitude of the revival, counter attack by the Adversary and resultant return of the Messiah Himself. In which case, only Isra'el would be saved. Rather than being arrogant and ignoring Isra'el or impotent and financially supporting them without sharing the Good News (because our power comes from Yeshua, not finances), we must be diligent in expressing our thanks to God for turning them over to disobedience so that all men could be saved by grace,[238] making us all family in the Kingdom. This gratitude must take the form of sharing with His people the only thing that can help them—Yeshua's deliverance—as we fulfill His purpose for Gentile believers, which is to provoke His people Isra'el to jealousy.

A Light to the Nations

God's plan for Gentiles to provoke His people Isra'el to jealousy is only Part B of an intricate plan for world reconciliation to Himself. Part A of that plan is for His people Isra'el to be a light to the nations. In Genesis 12:2, ADONAI says to Avraham, "I will make of you a great nation, I will bless you, and I will make your name great; and you are to be a blessing. I will bless those who bless you, but I will curse anyone who curses you; and by you all families of the earth will be blessed." In Genesis chapter 28, Ya'akov (Jacob) has a dream in which he sees a ladder extending from earth to heaven with angels ascending and descending upon it. ADONAI then speaks to him in verses 13 and 14 saying, "I am ADONAI, the God of Avraham your [grand]father and the God of Yitz'chak (Isaac). The land on which you are lying I will give to you and to your descendants. Your descendants will be as numerous as the grains of dust on the earth. You will expand to the west and to the east, to the north and to the south. By you and your descendants all the families of the earth will be blessed." And as we read in chapter 6 of this book out of Exodus 19:5-6, ADONAI says of His people Isra'el, "Now if you will pay careful attention to what I say and keep my covenant, then you will be my own treasure from among all the peoples, for all the earth is mine; and you will be a kingdom of cohanim (priests) for me, a nation set apart."

These and other Scriptures demonstrate for us God's intention that the children of Isra'el would be set apart to God and teach the rest of us here on earth to obey ADONAI's holy commands; this is what priests do, learn the ways of God and teach them to the people. This is a vital responsibility of every Jewish believer. If you are a child of Isra'el, the Body pf Messiah needs you to step into this role. `However, as mentioned above, it is only possible for the children of Isra'el to be priests throughout the world if you pay careful attention to what He says and keep His covenant. Jeremiah 31 describes the new covenant with Isra'el because the first was broken. "'For this is the covenant I will make with the house of Isra'el after those days,' says ADONAI. 'I will put my Torah (Law) within them and write it on their hearts; I will be their God, and they will be my people." Yeshua's teachings, deliverance and gift of the Ruach make it possible for the Torah to be written on our hearts. Therefore, Messianic Jews are called to serve as priests to the Gentiles in the world on behalf of ADONAI. Because you have been grafted back into the olive tree through God's grace[239] and filled with the Ruach HaKodesh, He is restoring you to your rightful positions in the Body of Believers and using you to restore order to the Body.

Gentile believers so desperately need teaching from God's people Isra'el. For though none of us, as believers, are bound by the Law, there are blessings associated with keeping the commands of God and curses for not keeping them.[240] As Yeshua desires to take individual believers and the Body as a whole to another level in Him, He requires greater sacrifice and obedience on our parts. Learning the commands in the Old Testament and viewing them with the Ruach teaches us more about the character of God and helps to complete our transformations into the image of the Messiah, who Himself is a child of Isra'el, came for the lost sheep of Isra'el[241] and is returning to Isra'el.[242]

Gentile believers need spiritual revelation of the Old Testament, cultural revelation of the New Testament, and prophetic revelation of occurrences in the world today. While many of us are receiving this directly from God, we still need the history and culture of our brethren, the children of Isra'el, taught to us from your perspective, so that we can mature in the Ruach and gain deeper understanding. This equips us, as well, to provoke your brothers and sisters, Isra'el, to jealousy and fulfills a deep need within us for revelation of the Word of God (for Jews demand miraculous signs and Greeks look for wisdom[243]).

Additionally, the restoration of the children of Isra'el to a position of honor within the Body is a prophetic sign of the end times. In Zechariah chapters 8 and 9, the prophet speaks of the first and second coming of the Messiah. The prophecies are intertwined, however, and it takes discernment to understand when God is using him to refer to the first coming and the second. In chapter 8, he prophesies about the restoration of Yerushalayim and Isra'el. Some of it describes the period after the return from Babylonian exile. However, much of it refers to the blessings the nation will experience when His people collectively receive the Jewish Messiah. Verses 20 through 23 of chapter 8 clearly speak of a time in our future because it reads,

> "ADONAI-Tzva'ot (the LORD of hosts) says, 'In the future, peoples and inhabitants of many cities will come; the inhabitants of one city will travel to another and say, "We must go to ask ADONAI's favor and consult ADONAI-Tzva'ot. I'll go too." Yes, many peoples and powerful nations will come to consult ADONAI-Tzva'ot in Yerushalayim and to ask ADONAI's favor.' ADONAI-Tzva'ot says, 'When that time comes, ten men will take hold—speaking all the languages of the nations—will grab hold of the cloak of a Jew and say, "We want to go with you, because we have heard that God is with you."'"

This Scripture clearly reveals that God will use His people Isra'el again to lead the nations to Himself. This prophecy has not yet come to pass; it clearly awaits an appointed time because the nations have not yet come to God's people begging to be led to God. The reconciliation of all Isra'el back to the Father through Yeshua the Messiah marks that time.

Chapter 9 continues listing the enemies of Isra'el and God's judgment against them. However, the prophecy then states that the enemies that were judged will turn to God. Verse 7 reads, "I will end their eating meat with its blood still in it, snatching the disgusting things from between their teeth. But the surviving remnant will belong to our God; it will be like a clan in Y'hudah (Judah); and 'Ekron will be like a Y'vusi (Jebusite)." In these times, as it is prophesied, God will cleanse the enemies of Isra'el by causing them to follow His commands. The command mentioned here is concerning draining all the blood from meat before cooking it.[244] The prophet then adds that the remnant from these enemy nations will live amongst the children of Isra'el like another tribe, like the Jebusites lived among the children of Isra'el in Yerushalayim.[245] This revelation speaks of times passed, but also times to come. Verse 8 makes that clear. "Then I will guard my house against armies, so that none will march through or return. No oppressor will ever again overrun them, for now I am watching with my own eyes." Isra'el has been ruled over by oppressors since the return from the Babylonian exile, even after the Messiah's First Coming. Hence these verses speak of the end times, the times we are now experiencing and will soon experience.

It is in these days that God is training His people Isra'el, namely Messianic Jews, to teach the nations to honor and obey Him. For two thousand years, Gentile believers have been under grace without much guidance and accountability. However, it is time for us all to step into our rightful positions as children of God. He is calling us to a new level of obedience, following the full example of our Messiah who not only observed the Tanakh (Old Testament), but fulfilled its true spiritual meaning. We too must receive revelation of the spiritual significance of every mitzvah (law) in the Bible and apply both the spiritual and physical mitzvot (laws) to our lives and relationships with the Messiah. Gentiles who look like the world will never provoke God's people Isra'el to jealousy. We must trade in our loose religion for zealous obedience of the Father. And this is not bondage; it is complete freedom to live life to its fullest measure:[246] life in financial prosperity, life in physical health, life in direct daily relationship with the Father through the Ruach HaKodesh. God created the earth and all creatures on it. He knows what it takes to make us healthy and prosperous. He has revealed it in the Torah (Law of Moses) and it has not changed.

The Ruach will lead us into this transformation, individually and collectively, but we must be taught so that He will have something to work with. If the Ruach tells a Gentile believer to celebrate the Passover, he needs to have a brother or sister with whom he regularly worships to help him follow God's stipulations in the Bible and receive the full blessing of the Passover for his household. To go to the next level, Gentile believers must know and understand ALL of the Word of God as well as the culture and history of God with the people of the Torah, the children of Isra'el.

Brothers and sisters who are children of Isra'el, we need you to step up to the challenge as well. Invite us to worship with you and join us in worship. We must come together without judgment and resentment. God transforms all of us in His timing and His ways. Christians can no longer fear being put into legalistic bondage if we worship with Messianic Jews, and Messianic Jews can no longer be offended by the often unorthodox ways in which Gentiles worship God. We must decide to teach each other and learn from each other. In this way, God can use us together to transform His Body and prepare the world for the Messiah's return.

Being Sent

When the Messiah sends us to share the Good News with the world or testify one to another, it's essential that we understand the big picture, God's grand vision for sending out His children. God has always intended that mankind would have dominion on the earth. [247] Adam and Havah (Eve) gave up that dominion in the Garden of Eden,[248] yet the Messiah came to reclaim the earth and all of God's creation for ADONAI's purposes. As Yeshua's brothers and sisters, we're to be used in that mission to restore the earth to its original form in creation. In Romans 8:19-21, Sha'ul states, "The creation waits eagerly for the sons of God to be revealed; for the creation was made subject to frustration—not willingly, but because of the one who subjected it. But it was given a reliable hope that it too would be set free from its bondage to decay and would enjoy the freedom accompanying the glory that God's children will have."

God assigns an individual mission to each believer; one that will line up with the Word of God and fit into the collective mission of a ministry. And since every ministry mission is focused on proclaiming the Good News and reclaiming man's dominion on earth, our individual missions will always include revealing other children of God, through the Great Commission, and reclaiming the earth, through spiritual warfare with Satan.[249] Our transformation into the image of the Messiah was never meant to be solely for our own benefit. Every trial, every transforming experience, brings us closer to fulfilling the purpose for which we were sent to this earth. In Romans 8:28, Sha'ul says, "Furthermore, we know that God causes everything to work together for the good of those who love God and are called in accordance with his purpose." That purpose is the individual mission He has for each of us, which of course contributes to the collective mission for the children of God to have dominion on earth. Transformation is the only way for us to fulfill that mission, so Sha'ul continues in verse 29, "because those whom he knew in advance, he also determined in advance would be conformed to the pattern of his Son, so that he might be the firstborn among many brothers."

    The Messiah is our model and He strengthens us all, yet He requires that we strengthen each other and model His character before our brothers and sisters as well. As their brethren, it's our responsibility to diligently search for them, faithfully share the Good News with them, continually pray for their deliverance, and allow God to use us in their transformation into the image of the Messiah. After all, someone refused to give up on us.

    Our desire to proclaim the Good News is greatest just after every transforming experience we have, because the excitement about the new thing God has done in us is very high. As people, we pretty much do what we want to do. So, I praise God that every spiritual victory and every transforming experience incites us to want to share with others how to overcome in the area God brought us through. As you'll recall reading above, Sha'ul knew the Scriptures and the Good News about the Messiah well but had been blinded to the truth by his sin. Hence, he was able to immediately respond to the fire Yeshua placed in him to proclaim the Good News. We too can tell those around us about the new deliverance, healing or revelation God gave us in order to transform us yet again. The more mature we are as believers and the more understanding we have of the Word of God, the more effective we'll be in using our testimony to inspire non-believers to accept Yeshua or believers to come to know Him better.

Yeshua knows that we'll face lots of challenges when we share the Good News. For this reason, He prepares us for what's to come. He uses other believers to teach us, train us, and prepare us for the potential dangers we'll face. This training builds us up in our trust in Him so that we won't question our own understanding of the Messiah when presented with someone who challenges our knowledge of Him or experiences with Him. Though Sha'ul was full of knowledge, he too needed to be guided by other believers. So, he spent several days with the disciples in Damascus BEFORE going out to proclaim the Good News.[250] Whether we share our testimonies with family members, friends, brothers and sisters in the Messiah, co-workers or strangers, we always face having our beliefs or experiences with Yeshua challenged. This isn't to be taken lightly. You may be able to stand firm if a stranger challenges you, but it may be a different story if your spouse or best friend does it.

As we share our testimonies with others, non-believers as well as believers, we've got to know that Satan will use whatever and whomever he can to shake our foundation. He'll start out with the truth, or something that sounds a lot like it, but all of his words will lead to one big lie about Yeshua. Whether the lie is that you are in rebellion because you are no longer practicing "religion as usual" or that you didn't hear from the Messiah what you thought you heard, the goal will always be to plant a seed of doubt within you. Remember, without faith, it is impossible to please to God.[251] So, stand firm in your trust in Him. If God wants to correct you, He'll send someone who's going to represent Him. They'll tell you the truth in love[252] for the purpose of bringing you closer to Yeshua, not to push you away. God will never use the Deceiver to send a message to one of His children.

When people close to us deny the truth of our testimony or new birth in Him, it can be frustrating, even heart-breaking.

However, we must remember that we're only vessels for God's use. He's their Father just as He is ours. All we need to do is share the truth with them and allow Him to do the rest, even if it takes years. Yeshua never forces Himself on anyone. Every person with whom He comes into contact is given the choice of following Him and applying ALL truth to their lives. Keeping this in mind, we have to resist the temptation to force an acceptance of His deliverance or a new level of anointing on people. We're not their saviors, Yeshua is. Arguing over the Bible or getting into debates over God's will is not from God.[253] Instead, present your new revelation about the Messiah humbly and peacefully, for the message of Yeshua is referred to as "the Good News of shalom (peace)."[254]

Sha'ul's message about Yeshua wasn't readily accepted either. Verse 21 of Acts chapter 9 reads, "All who heard him were amazed. They asked, 'Isn't he the man who in Yerushalayim was trying to destroy the people who call on this name? In fact, isn't that why he came here, to arrest them and bring them back to the head cohanim (priests)?'" The people either rejected the Good News from Sha'ul or they questioned his own deliverance. Just as Sha'ul's relationship with the Messiah was questioned, ours will be too.

When you talk to people in your life about Yeshua, they'll often remind you of who you were before He delivered you or even who you are now. Many people expect believers to immediately be transformed into the likeness of the Messiah and have no patience for us as God develops us. Sometimes I think they know God's requirements of us better than we do. They use our present shortcomings and past ways of life as excuses to reject the truth for themselves. In the book of Acts, this happened to Sha'ul too, but he didn't allow it to turn him around. He continued to faithfully proclaim the Good News.

Because Sha'ul was determined to persevere despite the disbelief of others and persecution he suffered, he continued to grow in Yeshua. Verse 22 in Acts chapter 9 reads, "But Sha'ul was being filled with more and more power and was creating an uproar among the Jews living in Damascus with his proofs that Yeshua is the Messiah." He was able to use the Old Testament Scriptures to prove to people that Yeshua is in fact the Messiah and He came to fulfill the Scriptures.[255] Sha'ul's ability to use the Word of God to prove the truth about Yeshua and the truth of his own testimony was indisputable.

We don't have to create a case for the Messiah; the Bible does that for us. All we need to do is become intimate with the Word of God, from Genesis to Revelation. God will always give us what we need in order to do His work, but we must be persistent in prayer[256] and Bible study,[257] we must allow ourselves to be taught,[258] and we must be patient as God develops us.[259] It's sinful for us to disobey God by refusing to share all that He has done and is still doing in our lives, but it can be harmful to us and others if we strike out BEFORE Yeshua sends us. Ask God where and when He's sending you; He'll tell you and prepare you.[260] Then believe Him to carry you to and through your mission in victory.

CHAPTER 10
SERVING THE BODY

"For just as there are many parts that compose one body, but the parts don't all have the same function; so there are many of us, and in union with the Messiah we comprise one body, with each of us belonging to the others. But we have gifts that differ and which are meant to be used according to the grace that has been given to us.--Romans 12:4-6a

When I was in third grade, the tip of my middle finger on my right hand was severed in an accident in the school bathroom. My best friend unintentionally closed the door on my finger at the place where the door is attached to the wall by its hinges. For some reason (that I've not been able to figure out), my elementary school had large, metal doors on the stalls and the wall between them was made out of a stone resembling marble. Hence, the wall and door attached to it were immovable. After tugging for some time, I panicked and ripped my finger out of the door only to find that the tip of it remained in the door jam.

This was a tragic incident for me because it left me without the use of my writing hand for months. So that I wouldn't fail third grade, I had to do my homework on tape recordings while in the hospital. I hated making those tapes, so I changed the way I write, which got me back to writing sooner. Adonai worked miraculously on my behalf and my fingertip eventually grew back (there were a lot of folks praying for me, praise God). However, to this day, I write with the pencil pressed against my ring finger instead of my middle finger and my handwriting still looks exactly like it did in third grade. I don't even attempt to write in cursive, and I have this lump on my ring finger from pens pressing hard against it. But the effect this incident had on me is nothing compared to what happened to my severed fingertip. It shriveled up, died and was thrown away. My fingertip was completely useless once detached from my body because it had no life. It was disconnected from the life-giving source within me.

Every believer is a member of the Body of the Messiah, just as my finger is a member of my body. Believers who are disconnected from the global Body of the Messiah become just as useless as my severed fingertip. In John 15:5-6, Yeshua says, "I am the vine and you are the branches. Those who stay united with me, and I with them, are the ones who bear much fruit; because apart from me you can't do a thing. Unless a person remains united with me, he is thrown away like a branch and dries up. Such branches are gathered and thrown into the fire, where they are burned up."

The Messiah continues in that same chapter to discuss the way we are to cooperate (as in operate together) in the Body of the Messiah. "If you keep my commands, you will stay in my love—just as I have kept my Father's commands and stay in his love. I have said this to you so that my joy may be in you, and your joy be complete. This is my command: that you keep on loving each other just as I have loved you. No one has greater love than a person who lays down his life for his friends."[261]

Through the Messiah's words in John chapter 15, we see the importance of remaining connected to Him, the life source. Yeshua also stresses the importance of true fellowship with other believers: that we love one another and be friends. This doesn't come by casual acquaintance. We must be just as connected to the Body of Believers as we are to the Messiah in our personal relationship with Him. We must commune with each other, learn and worship together, and benefit from each other's relationships with the Messiah.

In the Messiah's words, this connection with the Body of Believers will make our joy complete. So, we can only surmise that our joy will be incomplete if we don't cooperate with the other members of the Messiah's Body. Think of your own body, your hand can never reach its full potential without cooperating with your brain, lungs, heart, wrist, arm and other body parts. Similarly, we can't receive the fullness of joy in the Messiah without operating in conjunction with other believers. Only through true fellowship with believers as active members of the Body can we allow God to perfect the love of Yeshua in our hearts. "For if a person does not love his brother, whom he has seen, then he cannot love God, whom he has not seen."[262]

Additionally, our faith is dead as believers if we aren't contributing our unique gifts and experiences to the overall Body of the Messiah.[263] This spiritual death eventually leads us to a separation from God and back to the road headed for destruction. The Body of the Messiah suffers as well when we, its members, aren't functioning in the roles for which God created us. When I was dismembered by the loss of my fingertip, I was hindered in what I could do. I couldn't play piano, write, clean up behind myself, bathe myself, or even play outside until God healed me. In the same way, the Body of the Messiah is disabled when a member is not functioning correctly or is completely unattached.

At times, we all feel insignificant in the grand scheme of things, but only God knows how important we truly are in fulfilling His purpose for the Body of the Messiah. Imagine not having the use of one part of your body: an eye, a hand, a toe, or one muscle in your stomach. You may not have to imagine due to an experience you've had or are having right now. Either way, this analogy helps us to see the importance of parts we take for granted on our own body. Likewise, we take for granted the importance of the members of the Body of the Messiah as well, others and ourselves. Sha'ul discusses this in First Corinthians chapter 12. He states, "For indeed the body is not one part but many. If the foot says, 'I'm not a hand, so I'm not part of the body,' that doesn't make it stop being part of the body."[264] He goes on to say, "But as it is, God arranged each of the parts in the body exactly as he wanted them,"[265] and "Now you together constitute the body of the Messiah, and individually you are parts of it."[266]

When a member of our body is not functioning or is disconnected, other members of our body have to work overtime to compensate. As in my case, my ring finger had to compensate for the loss of my middle finger, and it still does. The rightful order of things, with regard to using my hand for writing, was never restored. Additionally, my productivity decreased because every member of my body was not functioning as it should. Somewhere deep down inside me is the ability to write beautifully in my own script. But because of my accident, I'm stuck with "chicken scratch," as my mother calls it.

Similarly, when you or I are absent or complacent in the Body of the Messiah, other members have to work even harder to get the mission accomplished, and some things are just left undone because the members ordained to function in those roles aren't doing so. God will sometimes raise up someone else in the place of the absent member (just like He allowed my fingertip to grow back), but the effects of the first member's absence will never be completely erased. What God has ordained for you to do can only be done by you, and the entire Body will suffer if you're not in your position.

Parts of the Body

It is ADONAI's will that all of His children exist in His image, in its fullness. Not one of us is currently capable of this, though, as none of us knows Him fully.[267] However, when believers come together with the specific gifts and anointing given to us by the Messiah, the Body is built up "until we all arrive at the unity implied by trusting and knowing the Son of God, at full manhood, at the standard of maturity set by the Messiah's perfection."[268]

For the Body of Believers to progress toward this fullness, we must allow the Ruach HaKodesh to remove dividing walls between denominations, ministries and individual believers, thus uniting the global Body of the Messiah. In First Corinthians 12:4-6, Sha'ul discusses ADONAI's intention to have diversity within the Body, not division. "Now there are different kinds of gifts, but the same Spirit gives them. Also, there are different ways of serving, but it is the same Lord being served. And there are different modes of working, but it is the same God working them all in everyone." The Ruach endows all believers with spiritual gifts to contribute to local congregations and the Body as a whole.[269] The Messiah births ministries and commissions ministers for varying types of service within the Body.[270] The Father reveals different modes of working to groups of us within the Body, to build up His

House made of many different stones, with one chief cornerstone holding it together—Yeshua.[271] By coming together, we display all of the gifts of the Spirit, every kind of service to the Messiah and the different workings of God.

Historically, many events have occurred within the Body to separate us. The destruction of Isra'el by the Roman Empire in 70 AD left the Body without a center. While based in Yerushalayim, believers had a place to connect with each other and our Jewish roots (since the community of believers was considered a sect of Judaism). Once decentralized, the spirit of paganism resurfaced in undelivered Gentile leaders within the Body and used them to infuse pagan rites and beliefs in with worship of the One True God; the culmination of which was the First Council of Nicea in 325 AD. To insure the false doctrine would be unchallenged, Jewish believers were executed or driven from the Body. Later, many Gentile believers felt a call back to Scripture and protested the current practices of the Church. However, without Jewish believers to teach historic and cultural revelations of Scripture, much of the Bible was misunderstood and thereby ignored. The protestors, separated by differing doctrines, then split into the Protestant denominations.

Denominationalism has scattered God's House. Fear of false doctrine infiltrating our congregations and unaddressed grievances with each other perpetuate this division. Denominationalism in the Body is probably the most damaging form of division because each group holds important revelation and experiences with God that the rest of us need to be whole. It was never the Father's intention that we would compare these revelations to exalt ourselves over each other, but rather, His will is that we come together and share our revelations. Doing so will reveal the Truth, in its fullness, and complete God's House. Living in one House would protect the Body from falsehood and develop unity and maturity among us.[272]

Instead of living together though, we often condemn each other and segregate ourselves. Yet, we would receive revelation and power that we have never before experienced if we allowed each group to minister to the rest of us that which God has given them. Seemingly opposing revelations often lead us to the narrow gate and hard road that lead to life. Allowing Messianic Jews to teach us to obey the Torah (Law of Moses) lines us up to receive a new level of blessings from God. In like manner, Charismatics demonstrate the power of being led by the Ruach, rather than ruled by legalism. These two are not opposed to each other, keeping Torah and being led by the Ruach. In fact, when brought together, believers experience revival that only obedience and spiritual power can birth.

Though God didn't create denominationalism, He did separate us into cultural and geographic groups to reveal Himself in various ways. Each group sees and experiences the Creator differently, thus denying any group of God's people is to deny God Himself. Yet appreciating all of God's people is not enough; we must also tell each other the truth in love.[273] For this, Matthew 18:15-20 is helpful on an individual and group level. If one group of believers espouses something other than the truth of the Word of God, leaders from another group should reveal this to leaders of the group in error. If the leaders refuse to listen, leaders from two or more groups should unite to reveal the truth again. If this is unproductive, leaders from various groups should come together to address the leaders in error. All of these discussions are held in private and only between leaders. If none of these attempts work, leaders throughout the Body should begin warring in prayer and fasting on behalf of the group in error.

We don't operate this way within the Body because we don't want anyone to correct us, so we don't correct others. However, Proverbs 17:10 reads, "A rebuke makes more impression on a person of understanding than a hundred blows on a fool." Additionally, Proverbs 16:21 states, "A wise-hearted person is said to have discernment, and sweetness of speech adds to learning." When we rebuke in love, we do not accuse or blame, we share the truth for the Messiah's sake, not our own. We also acknowledge that no lover of God would intentionally teach false doctrine but must have learned it incorrectly themselves and are possibly in a stronghold. We then offer ourselves to God to assist in any way He sees fit, recognizing our own need for correction and accepting any correction lovingly offered to us in return.

Division between groups of believers is not the only form of disunity within the Body. Within the same denominations and geographic areas, ministries are disconnected, missing the opportunity to serve the Messiah together. Throughout the New Testament, many ministries were formed. However, they all supported each other, demonstrating true oneness. When one ministry was in need, another responded, not just through sending an offering,[274] but many times by sending laborers.[275] In so doing, all ministries benefited from the strengths of all others and service to the Messiah was complete.

Each ministry ordained by God represents a portion of the Messiah's identity and purpose. The name of a ministry (just as the name of a person) reveals God's divine purpose for the ministry and who that group is within the Body. Each ministry is a part of an organ or limb of the Messiah. For example, if the name of your ministry has "Worship Center" in it, you are a part of the heart of the Messiah that demonstrates love to God's people and worships the Father. If your ministry name has "Deliverance" in it, you are part of the Messiah's hand that reaches out and takes hold of sheep drowning in sin. Worship centers and deliverance ministries need to function together because the sheep that are snatched from the fire need to feel the love of the Messiah and be taught to worship Him.

Sadly, many ministries do not have a sense of identity and purpose in the Body, so they continue to plan worship services and programs lacking life and power. In such cases, the glory of the Messiah is not revealed through them as He ordained. Even growth and expansions of territory should always center around the original identity and purpose of the ministry. Many ministries are currently suffering because they watch others and attempt to minister like other congregations. However, the thriving ministries are those that understand who they are and what they were birthed to do in the Body. They are constantly being transformed through continually learning, growing and changing, so that they will never stop bearing fruit.

God blesses those who are willing to be a blessing to others. This is not just true for individuals but also for ministries. If your ministry sees itself as just one piece of the greater Body of Believers and works hard to uplift the Messiah as that one piece, He will connect your ministry with others that need to learn how to serve the Messiah as you do. The other ministries will also provide an anointing and experience, through the kind of service to which they have been called, that is lacking in your own ministry.

This is how we function as a Body, without fear, selfishness or confusion. A ministry that is functioning as Yeshua ordained is too busy serving Him, His way, to get caught up in internal strife and external competition. Members of these types of ministries are more mature and developed and the leaders rest assured, knowing they are good and faithful servants of the Most High.

For a believer to be a good and faithful servant, she must receive and faithfully exercise the spiritual gifts the Ruach has given.[276] All of us have been given gifts to use in God's service.[277] It is those of us who do not esteem ourselves too highly who recognize that we are just stewards of these gifts, and we, as well as our spiritual gifts, belong to the one Body.[278] Everything the Ruach places in me belongs to you, and all that the Ruach has done in you belongs to me. The one Messiah died for the sins of all, and all who accept the benefits of His sacrifice, our soul salvation, are grafted into the one Body. Not until each individual believer starts to see herself as a part of one whole will the Body come together as one.

Connecting to the Body

In verse 26 of Acts chapter 9, we read that Sha'ul went to Yerushalayim and tried to join the disciples there. He didn't return to the Sanhedrin, not even to resign his position as a Parush (Pharisee). Instead, he tried to join the Body of Believers that was already established. Though he had seen the Messiah in the flesh and proclaimed the Good News boldly, he recognized his need to be connected to the Body of Believers. They were, of course, distrustful of his true motives.

So, God sent Bar-Nabba (Barnabas) to speak on his behalf to the other disciples and present him to the leaders among the believers: the emissaries (apostles). Sha'ul stayed there with them and boldly proclaimed the Word of God in the name of Yeshua.

You and I recognize the awesome tasks God had in store for Sha'ul, and he may have been somewhat aware of this himself at the time. This didn't keep him from recognizing that he needed to be joined to the larger Body of the Messiah though. When he went forth in Damascus proclaiming the Good News, he and others realized that he had a tremendous gift, thus he began to develop a following and a ministry. Whether they agreed with what he said or not, everyone who heard him knew that he had a gift to boldly proclaim the Good News and to explain the Scriptures in such a way that people would see Yeshua in them.

Such a gift can be overwhelming, even frightening, but it can also become a source of pride. Because Sha'ul had sinned so greatly against Yeshua, yet He still appeared to him to save his soul, Sha'ul was forever humbled by this experience. He would never allow himself to get proud of the gift God had given him, and he recognized that it was given to him for one reason: the edification of the Body of the Messiah that it may bring glory to God. He knew, beyond a shadow of a doubt, that he had to connect himself to the other believers God had called to serve and represent the Messiah.

As believers, we can't afford to see ourselves as anything but servants to Yeshua. However, we must be transformed into servants and an attitude of servitude can only fully develop when we're committed to fellowship in the global Body of Believers. Now let me tell you, nobody on earth will test your love, patience, endurance and overall character like believers. God uses us to press each other out and that is not always pretty. But as servants, we must be obedient to our master's example and charge, which is to love one another. And as family, we must stick together no matter what. If I love my brother, then I will allow God to use me in his life and him in mine. There is no better way to be used by God than in His House with His children.

It would be disobedient and proud of any of us to believe that we can fulfill God's purpose for our lives without the other members of the Body of the Messiah working with us. One member of any body cannot function alone. Neither can one limb of a body, such as represents a ministry or denomination. We don't just fulfill a mission together; we also help each other grow. The hand washes the foot and the foot propels the rest of the body. It would also be an affront to the Word of God to think that we aren't needed in the overall Body of the Messiah. My God is wise; He's a strategist. When He does things, it's usually to serve a three-fold purpose. Saving each one of us wasn't just so that 1) we wouldn't be separated from God eternally; it was also that we could 2) be used in the lives of His other children to 3) restore the world to its rightful order under the dominion of man worshipping the one sovereign LORD.

Being an active part of a local body of believers helps us grow up into the person God created us to be. The local body is the place where we're able to flex our spiritual muscles and get a feel for how those bad boys work, whether in the pew or pulpit. It is in this setting that we get the teaching, correction and fellowship that we need to walk in the likeness of the Messiah. It's wonderful to be a part of an international ministry or overseas missions, but each of us needs to be connected to a local congregation to get what we need practically and to contribute directly to what God is doing in the world around us. Mass media (in the forms of televangelism, broadcast messages, books, etc.) is used by God to be a supplement to the activities of the local body and a connector to the global Body of the Messiah. It should never be a substitute for commitment to a local branch of Zion. Even if God has called you to lead an international ministry, there should always be a congregation at the place where you call home that supports you and that you support. Staying connected builds "family skills" in you and tests those skills as well as your commitment to family. As representatives of Yeshua, we are relationship and covenant makers, not breakers.

The Body Builds Believers

In chapter 1, we briefly discussed Adonai's transformation of the Body of the Messiah in preparation for His return. I shared with you that Adonai is restoring order and authority to the Body. The order is being restored through the restoration of the children of Isra'el to their rightful place in His Body. The authority, however, is being restored through the resurgence of five-fold ministry. Turn with me to Ephesians chapter 4. Verses 4-7 read, "There is one body and one Spirit, just as when you were called you were called to one hope. And there is one Lord, one trust, one immersion, and one God, the Father of all, who rules over all, works through all and is in all. Each one of us, however, has been given grace to be measured by the Messiah's bounty."

The text goes on to discuss the Messiah giving gifts to us at His ascension. These ascension gifts are listed in verse 11, which reads, "Furthermore, he gave some people as emissaries, some as prophets, some as proclaimers of the Good News, and some as shepherds and teachers." It's not a coincidence that these gifts were given at Adonai's ascension, because it will take these gifts to prepare the Body of the Messiah to be called up with Him at the time of His return.[279]

These are not the only spiritual gifts given to believers, but these are distinct ascension gifts. Believers with these gifts are often called five-fold ministers. In most cases, five-fold ministers are given one dominant gift from among these gifts. Yeshua makes this particular gift the area in which they're commissioned as well. However, He also develops other gifts in that believer to be a better representation of Yeshua and available to fill many needs in the Body of the Messiah as they arise. Yet, the emissary Sha'ul refers to believers with specific commissions in Ephesians, rather than just gifts. Those who are commissioned in these roles then become gifts to the whole Body.

Yeshua functioned in all five of these commissions during His ministry on earth. The global Body of the Messiah is called to follow His example, so it must function fully in five-fold ministry. The local body should be a microcosm of the global

Body. It should be culturally diverse, abounding in spiritual gifts, which we'll discuss later, and fulfilling each and all of the ascension commissions. These five commissions make the Body of Believers whole and develop maturity in the individual believer. Other verses in Ephesians chapter 4 make it clear to us the importance of each of the five ascension commissions in the global body, the local body, and more specifically, in the life of the believer.

Emissaries (Apostles)

The emissary is listed first; he or she serves as an overseer in the Body of the Messiah and an establisher of new congregations. Emissaries insure that every branch of Zion is built upon the foundation of the Messiah. Therefore, God has given us authority to build up and to tear down, to plant and to uproot. We're charged with getting Adonai's House in order. We have natural characteristics and skills that direct people into their God-ordained places, correct error within the Body of the Messiah, and develop power in individuals and congregations. For this, and many other reasons, we are the commanders in God's army as we lead the Body into aggressive spiritual warfare.

The order of the five-fold ministers listed in Ephesians 4:11 is not a ranking, but it is the order in which Adonai dispatches us when He desires to reclaim a region here on earth for His Kingdom. Emissaries are sent first, hence our title (the definitions of emissary and apostle are the same—"one sent forth on a mission"). We go into a region currently under the oppression of demonic forces and begin to war aggressively against those forces in the region. We tear down mindsets, spiritual strongholds, even political systems designed to oppress. Yeshua has given us a specific anointing to fight evil spirits that are on the highest levels of command in the Adversary's army, so we are commissioned on the highest level in God's army.

Emissaries also connect the local body to the global Body through national and international missions and by inciting fellowship between congregations, due to our burden for the universal Body of the Messiah. We remind the local congregation that God is moving throughout the world and that the local body is an important part of God's international work, especially now that we're in the end times. This magnifies the significance of EACH believer in the world. Verses 4 through 6 of Ephesians chapter 4 then become somewhat of a mantra for the emissary. "There is one body and one Spirit, just as when you were called you were called to one hope. And there is one Lord, one trust, one immersion, and one God, the Father of all, who rules over all, works through all and is in all." These verses are like a banner that emissaries hold up to remind the Body that there is a bigger picture, a greater work of which we are all a part.

Prophets

Prophets hear the Voice of God and speak His timely and specific words to His people. The words of the prophets are God's truth. They are not and cannot be opinion or even wisdom. A prophet is a megaphone, an instrument to magnify God's Voice. Because we're only translating what we see and hear in the spiritual realm into the physical realm, every prophetic word spoken should line up with the Holy Scriptures. If it doesn't, it either didn't come from God or it was tainted by flesh. We serve the same functions the prophets of the Tanakh (Old Testament) served, yet we must operate through the grace of God and demonstrate the love of Yeshua, as we survive only by grace and love ourselves. Our words should never be spoken in judgment or condemnation of believers, but for the purpose of warning against falling into judgment and directing to the path God has lain out.

This is essential in our role in spiritual warfare as we reclaim areas for the Kingdom here on earth. Prophets come after the emissaries to convict people of sin. Once Yeshua has torn down spiritual strongholds, evil political systems and other forms of oppression in the lives of people, they are then in a position to truthfully evaluate their sins. As we discussed in chapter 2, people in strongholds cannot take honest inventories of their spiritual condition because all information they receive will be filtered through the stronghold (either spiritual or political). Yet once the anointing of the emissary has been used to uproot these false doctrines and implant truth, the prophet can then be dispatched to convict according to the truth. Demonstrating God's grace and love are important here because the next phase is proclaiming the Good News. People should be ready to hear about the redemptive power of Yeshua rather than condemned to feel that there's no hope for them.

Prophets may prophesy to nations, congregations or individuals. The focus of the prophecy is determined only by God and cannot be limited, neither minimized nor maximized, by man. Prophets help local bodies and believers mature in the Messiah by pointing to God's specific will and timing in various situations. This includes identifying ministry callings, inquiring of God about major congregational decisions, and leading congregations and believers to confess hidden sins. In the global Body of Messiah, God uses prophets to illuminate the direction He's taking us in, to reveal new strategies in defeating spiritual wickedness in high places, to predict the coming moves of God, and to uncover sinful trends in the Body. Verse 15 in Ephesians chapter 4 perfectly sums up God's purpose for prophets. "Instead, speaking the truth in love, we will in every respect grow up into him who is the head, the Messiah."

Proclaimers of the Good News (Evangelists)

Proclaimers of the Good News reach outside of the walls of the congregation to bring in new believers. They insure that the congregation never forgets to share the Good News of Yeshua's death, burial and resurrection to those who may have never heard it or need to hear it again. Proclaimers of the Good News also keep the body involved in the community by caring for the spiritual and physical needs of those who are not members, as demonstrations of God's loving care are just as important as sharing the Good News about God's loving care through Yeshua.

In reclaiming regions for the Kingdom, evangelists share the Good News of Yeshua with the people in the region who have been recently delivered from strongholds and convicted of sins. They must be prepared with the message of salvation for people struggling under the conviction of God. Without hearing, understanding and receiving the redemption that comes from our risen Savior, unbelievers who have come to the knowledge that their sins lead them to death will be left to be devoured by the enemy. His trap of condemnation will convince them that they've been good-for-nothing from the start and that God doesn't love them. Proclaimers of the Good News must then share the truth of God's grace and mercy through the sacrifice of His Son, but also empower individuals to allow that love to flow into every area of their lives, thus transforming them into the people God originally intended them to be. Highlighting God's deep desire that each person be saved and proclaiming that He has a purpose for every human life will inspire new believers to put in the hard work of surrendering their wills to God's will for their lives.

Verses 12 and 13 of Ephesians chapter 4 describe the goal the evangelist is always working toward: "Their task is to equip God's people for the work of service that builds the body of the Messiah, until we all arrive at the unity implied by trusting and knowing the Son of God, at full manhood, at the standard of maturity set by the Messiah's perfection." The evangelist does this through pressing us toward the fulfillment of the Great Commission in Matthew 28:19-20 as we discussed in the last chapter. Congregations without proclaimers of the Good News will always appear to be dead, lacking growth and movement. This happens because the evangelist helps to ensure that we add works to our faith. And you know what Ya'akov (James) said about faith without works: it's dead.[280]

Shepherds

The shepherds are most often rabbis or pastors in local congregations. Five-fold ministers called to this commission represent the Good Shepherd[281] as they dispatch their duties. Many congregations today lack order and the shepherd is overworked because the other four ascension commissions are not serving effectively or the other ascension gifts are not in operation at all. The shepherd is responsible for caring for God's people once they come into the local body. He or she must be an example of Yeshua to the body of believers and demonstrate Messiah-like love and leadership.

In reclaiming territories, shepherds are sent after proclaimers of the Good News to care for new believers and protect them from the Adversary. Under the direction of Adonai and the leadership of an emissary, shepherds develop a congregation out of a group of new believers. Congregations that are established before the apostolic anointing tears down strongholds and the prophetic anointing convicts of sin are often weak in their foundations, because members and ministers are still under invisible forms of oppression and unaware of the serious implications of their sins.

As an example of the Messiah, the shepherd is charged with verse 16 in Ephesians chapter 4. "Under his control, the whole body is being fitted and held together by the support of every joint, with each part working to fulfill its function; this is how the body grows and builds itself up in love." God uses the shepherd to support the development of individual believers so that we may become mature, contributing members of the whole Body of the Messiah. He insures that each member feels significant to the local body and continues to grow in her relationship with the Messiah. The shepherd creates a loving and nurturing environment for the sheep while counseling and training them for living as disciples of Yeshua in all areas of their lives. Shepherds help the sheep reach maturity and even send them off into their own ministries or missions when they are mature. A shepherd is the head of the local body by overseeing ministries through that particular congregation and training all ministers and members in the congregation.

Believers called to be shepherds are easy to spot because they demonstrate self-sacrificing love in everything they do. As five-fold ministers, shepherds team with evangelists to keep the welfare of individual believers at the forefront of the other five-fold ministers' minds. Because emissaries are so focused on the big picture, they often lose sight of the importance of caring for individual sheep. And prophets hear God's words of judgment and correction so much that frustration with individual believers easily sets in. As five-fold ministers come together to clean up the House of God, shepherds and evangelists remind all others to be sensitive to the needs and circumstances of individual believers so that the babies aren't thrown out with the bathwater.

Teachers

Teachers work tirelessly to insure that every member of the local congregation grows up in his knowledge of the Word of God. Teachers want individual believers to have a solid foundation in Scripture, which will guard them against false teachings and false prophets in these last and evil days. The teacher feeds new believers spiritual milk, that is Biblical teachings on an elementary level, until they're prepared for solid food, or more complex Biblical teachings. Teachers adapt their teaching styles and content as believers develop in their relationships with the Messiah.[282]

As we reclaim regions for the Messiah, the teacher works with the shepherd to train up the new believers. She is most directly responsible for ensuring that the minds of the sheep are renewed. After strongholds have been torn down, new teaching is essential. The teacher lays a foundation in the minds of babes in the Messiah that will propel them on their spiritual journeys with Yeshua. Teachers also instill a deep desire for and appreciation of personal Bible study and prayer. Teachers want disciples of Yeshua to develop wisdom, spiritual strength and a sound doctrine.

A teacher is able to "correctly handle the word of truth,"[283] so she knows what Scriptures to teach according to the season and development of the local congregation and its members. Hence, verse 14 in Ephesians chapter 4 serves as the goal for all teachers. "We will then no longer be infants tossed about by the waves and blown along by every wind of teaching, at the mercy of people clever in devising ways to deceive."

Five-fold teachers have a burning desire to know and explain Scripture to the Body. They are interested in making sure that believers, individually and collectively, incorporate all of God's words, with His original intent in mind, into our lives and ministry. Hence, five-fold teachers CANNOT operate in their commission without being filled with the Ruach HaKodesh. Without this person of the Trinity, one is merely a theologian and in the position to do a lot of harm to new believers and the Body as a whole as Scripture is interpreted by the carnal mind rather than through the Spirit of the Holy God.[284]

Among the five-fold ministers, the teacher keeps the ministers and members grounded in the Word of God, who is Yeshua[285] and tests all things against the Bible. While spiritual revelation and anointing are essential in reclaiming territory and restoring order to God's House, everything must line up with that which God has already spoken in His Word. On the five-fold ministry team, teachers keep the Word of God in the forefront of everyone's minds. The teacher insures that apostles tear down strongholds through the authority of Yeshua, by the power of His Word, and never drift into pride and personal authority. The teacher checks prophecies against the Word to be sure they aren't tainted or false. She also feeds the evangelist the Word as a tool to use along with personal testimony when sharing the Good News. Lastly, the teacher works with the pastor to make sure that ministries are birthed according to the Word, and thus built on the solid foundation of Yeshua.[286]

Identifying five-fold ministers

Lately, I've heard a lot of talk in the Body of the Messiah about "titles." Because we as believers have become so proud and covetous regarding our "positions" in the Body, the Adversary has been able to use leaders in the Body to oppress Adonai's flock (I say Adonai's flock because the people don't belong to the leaders; we're just stewards). This then has made many believers want to stray away from any type of title to avoid pride and strife. However, every extreme mindset comes from the Adversary.[287] Remember, Yeshua said that a narrow gate and a hard road lead to eternal life, and few find it. Temperance is an important virtue for us as believers to learn. That being said, we must identify the names and ranks of the spirits with which we're fighting in a region. Yet we must also have the boldness to identify our names and commissions to each other and to the Adversary. Otherwise, there will be confusion, timidity and delusion in the Body of the Messiah, tactics Satan uses to scatter us.

You may currently be a priest, ministry leader, cantor, worship leader, lay person in a congregation or any other member of the Body of the Messiah, yet Yeshua is clearly calling you to serve as a five-fold minister. Identifying yourself as a five-fold minister is essential in the development of the global Body of the Messiah. There is a growth process for each commission, so I wouldn't suggest a self-proclamation before man and God at this point, but you do need some accountability. You need to pray about this, accept in your heart that the Messiah is moving you in this direction, and then share that with a trusted and knowledgeable spiritual leader in your life.

If you don't have a spiritual leader, or your spiritual leader knows less than you do about five-fold ministry, pray and ask God to send you to the right person to whom you may be accountable. This person will pray with you and help to develop you into this calling. As God moves in you, he will remind you to have faith in God and bring back to your remembrance all you have shared that God has told you. This will be essential when the enemy tries to make you doubt your calling, through fear within yourself or even persecution within the Body.

Every commission we receive requires proper training and its own transformation experience. Yes, there is a transformation for every commission we receive. However, you must also receive confirmation from God and people who walk in spiritual authority to fully exercise the calling of your commission. Don't worry. God will always send other believers to confirm the call on your life, but it will happen when you're ready to walk out your commission. Once this has occurred, walk in your calling as a five-fold minister and boldly proclaim that this is the commission in which the Messiah has sent you. Our example of Sha'ul is an excellent one here because he always identified himself as the emissary Sha'ul.[288]

He wasn't being arrogant because just before or after that he would say something like "by God's will" or "a slave of the Messiah Yeshua." We must be like him in this because the warfare is fierce. Believers and demons need to hear us proclaim who we are in the Messiah.

Turn to Acts 19:13-17. In this text, the seven sons of a Jewish high priest (which means they themselves were priests) tried to cast out a demon by stating, "I exorcise you by the Yeshua that Sha'ul is proclaiming!" The demon then replied to them, "Yeshua I know. And Sha'ul I recognize. But you? Who are you?" Then he whipped their tails and ran them out of the house naked and bleeding. This scenario demonstrates for us the importance of not trying to walk in someone else's commission or minister before we are prepared, but more importantly that even the demons knew who Sha'ul was. They knew because he identified his name and his commission in every region to which the Messiah sent him. Demons had gotten the news about him and were on the lookout for the emissary Sha'ul. We too can walk in the same type of authority if we are obedient enough to accept our call and commission from Yeshua, humble enough to allow Him to transform us, patient enough to wait for confirmation and bold enough to proclaim our commission in the earthly and the heavenly realms[289] once He sends us out.

The individual believer benefits from the fulfillment of the five-fold commissions in the local body, as Yeshua expects all of us to become mature enough to help fulfill the commands to the Body of the Messiah, given through Sha'ul, in Ephesians 4:4-16. The emissary, prophet, proclaimer of the Good News, shepherd and teacher are not the only members of the Body who are required to fulfill this charge. We all are. However, the Body of the Messiah benefits from having specific people who are called to be champions, if you will, of a certain part of this charge. This keeps the Body of Believers focused on representing Yeshua in His fullness, not just in part. Now that God is restoring five-fold ministry, the Body of the Messiah will experience a power and anointing that surpasses even that which is described in the book of Acts.

This brief look at the five-fold commissions paints a picture for us of the importance of working together in the Body of the Messiah. Some of us are called to fill one of these commissions as God develops other gifts in us. Others in the Body may be filled with one or more of the ministry and motivational gifts listed in Romans 12 and 1 Corinthians 12. We'll discuss those in a moment. Whatever calling and gifts you have, remember that the Messiah was the only man who could embody every characteristic of the Father within Himself. So, each of us will have the gifts and walk in the commissions for which God created us, not someone else. This is reason enough for us to stay connected to the Body of the Messiah, because none of us can function effectively alone.

Serving the Local Body

As believers we are a part of the global Body of Believers, but we must serve the needs of the local body too. We must give to the local body of believers our material possessions, our time and our abilities. Ministry begins at home. The disciples were sent to Yerushalayim, Y'hudah (Judea), Shomron (Samaria), and then the ends of the earth.[290] And even while out on missions elsewhere, Sha'ul continually took up collections for the body in Yerushalayim[291] and reported his successes and challenges to the body there.[292] Just as God uses the local body to bless our lives, He uses us to bless the local body. Unwillingness on our parts to be a blessing to the local body is disobedience to God, and it's just plain selfish. Selfishness is NOT a characteristic of the Messiah. Hence, the call to bless the local body doesn't just benefit the congregation or ministry, but it also makes us more like the Messiah.

The opposite of selfish is selfless or self-sacrificing. Now we know that IS a characteristic of the Messiah. It's important to note, from the beginning, that serving the needs of the local body is going to be a sacrifice. That sacrifice may include sharing the resources and expertise of your international ministry with that small ministry that brought you up or committing to serve in a ministry in your local church or synagogue. Either way, Yeshua calls us to sacrifice for the local body by serving its needs. That's the only way that God can use serving as a means to press out worldly characteristics in us and pour in godly ones. Not everything God calls us to do for the Body of the Messiah is going to be convenient and easy. It wouldn't benefit us if it were. Instead, God uses serving others as a way to challenge us and grow us up as believers and as people.

A good way to begin breaking ourselves of our selfishness towards God is to commit our material possessions to Him. Believers should devote everything we have to God's service: our homes, cars, money, clothing, all of it. That means a total surrender of our material goods, those things we've worked all our lives to amass. We can only do this by living Matthew 6:33. "But seek first his Kingdom and his righteousness, and all these things will be given to you as well." We should be more concerned about the things of God than the things of this world and willing to sacrifice them all for His purpose and glory.

None of us start our walk with Yeshua having this attitude, especially in this society. Yet the sad truth is that even after years of claiming Him as our Lord and Deliverer many of us still don't develop an attitude of sacrifice. That's another opportunity for transformation. The most widely quoted Scripture on this topic is Malachi 3:6-15. In this Scripture, God accuses the children of Isra'el of robbing Him in tithes and offerings. Up to this point in Malachi, ADONAI had been admonishing the priests. Here He admonishes everyone, and the priests are still included. We owe God our tithes, the first tenth of our income, for the building up of His kingdom. They pay the bills of the sanctuary and they finance the ministries. An offering is a financial or material gift we give to God, above our tithes. Hence, we can't actually give an offering until we have given our tithes. Our faithfulness in this area is essential to building up the Kingdom of God here on earth.

After we line up with the simple commandments of God about giving tithes and offerings, we must then allow Him to take us even further. If you are a member of a local body, give more than you feel is "required" of you. If you lead a thriving ministry, pour into a struggling local ministry. If you're concerned about their financial management, then loan them your accountant for a few months—free of charge—or give them some free financial management training sessions, one-on-one with the leaders. In this way, we function as a whole body, leaving nothing undone and no one behind.

Just like anything else in this world, the Body of the Messiah can't function without money. God doesn't want the Body to become like the world and be overly concerned about how to raise funds because this will taint the Word of God that goes forth; it also demonstrates a lack of faith. Instead, He shares His riches with the servants of God, so that we can give back to the Body and allow His resources to be used to build His Kingdom. Hence, giving presses self-will and stinginess out of us to birth obedience and sacrifice in us. Even as ministry leaders, we often become stingy. Because of the pressures of being responsible for a part of the Body, many times we fail to pour out of our ministry into other ministries for fear that God won't replace the resources. But Malachi 3 applies to individuals and ministries. Just keep pouring, in accordance to what the Ruach is telling you, and watch God work.

Additionally, giving requires that we take a more careful look at our own financial situation. This brings us closer to living "life in its fullest measure" as the Messiah promised us.[293] Every promise includes work that we must do to position ourselves to receive from God. The work in that promise regarding finances has to do with allowing God to transform us into good stewards over our finances. No matter who we are, how old we are, or how much money we make, God wants to direct the use of our finances. He doesn't want His money to go toward building up the Adversary's kingdom. Some things we just don't need. Other things we don't need right now. Either way, money management is important in developing us into the people God would have us to be.

The only thing harder for mature adults to sacrifice than money is time. We're very selfish about it, protective even. For this very reason, giving our time to the local body is an important requirement for true believers because that "time stinginess" is pressed out of us. In every body of believers, there are ministries that need the support of the members and outside ministries. Whether you are a member of a local body and feel led to join a ministry in your congregation, or you are a ministry leader and feel led to support local bodies, God will always honor your sacrifice of time and restore it to you 100-fold, provided you follow all of His instructions to you about being a good steward of your time.

Spending time in fellowship with believers in the local body is also essential to our own growth because we can learn to change our lives and attitudes in ways that will break Satan's hold upon us and bring us closer to God. Sometimes it's hard to commit to a congregation or develop a covenant between ministries, because people who are constantly being pressed out can fight against the press and become quite volatile. But God knows that even the quirks and issues found in every congregation can also be used to press out believers (that's you and me, not the other people). Join a local body if you're not a member of one, and stay there (unless God moves you) so that you can learn commitment to serving others, obedience to God, patience with His people and seeing the perfected work of Yeshua in His imperfect disciples. After all, that's what Yeshua saw when He called you and me.

If you are a ministry leader or shepherd, commit yourself to the ministry to which God has called you (even when there is no one there but you and your spouse). Giving up on what God has birthed through you to go to another ministry where they can pay you a salary is just like leaving your child on the street because he has special needs and going to adopt a healthy child. If your ministry is not healthy, petition God about it. Healthy ministries, just like healthy children, start with healthy parents. Let Him transform you, again, so that He can transform your ministry. Then it will increase in health as you do, because you will know better how to nurture it. If you lead a healthy ministry, sacrifice some of your time to assist your brothers and sisters tend the branch of Zion for which they are responsible. They may not be as good at pruning as you are and in need of some encouragement and support before they consider giving up.

The next thing God requires of us is that we serve the Body of the Messiah through our abilities. Our gifts and talents are not our own; they belong to God, because "every good act of giving and every perfect gift is from above."[294] Some of us are given one of the ascension gifts discussed earlier. Others of us have ministry or motivational gifts. Sha'ul discusses some of these gifts in 1 Corinthians chapter 12. There in verse 7, he says, "Moreover, to each person is given the particular manifestation of the Spirit that will be for the common good," once again affirming that everyone who has accepted Yeshua the Messiah as their Lord and Deliverer has been given a spiritual gift to be used in the Body of the Messiah.

He then mentions a few of the gifts: wisdom, word of knowledge, faith, healing, working of miracles, prophecy, judging between spirits, speaking in tongues and interpreting tongues. In verse 28 of that chapter, he adds the gifts of helps and administration. Additionally, in Romans 12:7-8 he adds serving, teaching, counseling, giving, leading and mercy. And the Psalms are full of expressions about using musical gifts to praise God. God has given you a gift for the use of the Body of the Messiah. Whether it's an ascension gift, a ministry gift, or a motivational gift, God has uniquely gifted you in one of these areas that you might build up other believers and help establish His Kingdom on earth.

Now all abilities and gifts must be developed, and the bearer must be equipped to use them. Our bodies, minds and spirits have to be trained to first recognize our gifts, then develop our gifts, and lastly devote them to God's intended purpose for them. Serving the needs of the local body helps us to do all three. God sends His children to congregations that need the particular abilities we have, and He sends ministries to other ministries that need the particular anointing we have. He's not going to waste His gifts, so He strategically places us in a body, or in relationship with a body, that needs exactly what we have to offer. He also places us in a body, or in relationship with a body, that has what we need. We just have to make sure God has led us to the ministry rather than us choosing it because of friends and family members or because it's in a convenient location.

Now don't get me wrong, serving a local body is better than not serving a body at all. However, serving a ministry outside of God's will for you is like being married to the person who's not ordained for you: you can't expect all of God's blessings and favor when you're not within His perfect will for your life. It also puts you in a position to miss out on God's perfect will when it shows up. You may not find your place in a synagogue or a church that's not the one God has chosen for you. Your anointing and revelation may not be received by a ministry that God hasn't ordained for you to be in relationship with. But unlike a marriage, you can go to God for guidance and change membership or relationship, as long as it's in God's will for you to do so. I would never suggest leaving a body of believers if God hasn't explicitly told you to do it. That's disobedience, and there are serious consequences for it. Difficulty and strife within a body of believers should NOT be construed as God's sign to leave, give up or break ties. It might just be your fire immersion. Seek God and He will answer you.

God's ordained purpose for our lives will always fit into God's mission for the ministry to which He has assigned us. He may use us outside of the Body of the Messiah in mighty ways, but He'll always desire for us to use what He gave us in His House as well. He's a jealous God and doesn't want the things He gave us to be used to bring glory to anyone but Him. He won't share His glory with us, Satan, a job or even a community organization. Our active contribution to a local body allows every area of our lives to bear everlasting fruit for the Kingdom of God. However, our disconnection from the Body of the Messiah only brings temporary glory to us.

Sha'ul understood this, that's why he tried to join the disciples in Yerushalayim. He was doing a great and powerful work for the Messiah OUTSIDE of the Body of Believers and the only thing people talked about was Sha'ul, how he proclaimed the Good News and how he had changed. They were so focused on Sha'ul that they tried to kill him. However, once he connected with the other believers and submitted to the leadership Yeshua had already established, he moved about freely in Yerushalayim and spoke boldly in the name of

Adonai.[295]   Once again, Sha'ul's life became endangered, but this time all of the believers were able to come together and allow God to tell them what they should do. Sha'ul was then sent out of Isra'el to protect him. This began his first missionary journey, which led to his commission as the emissary to the Gentiles.[296]

Using our talents to serve the needs of the Body of the Messiah is an important part of fulfilling God's purpose for our lives, and allowing our ministries to serve other ministries makes the Body whole. We've been redeemed by the Messiah, and we're designed to be joined to Him and each other. There are two Scriptural passages below that describe very clearly the relationship between being a part of the Body of Believers and being redeemed by Yeshua.

> "But I want you to understand that the head of every man is the Messiah, and the head of a wife is her husband, and the head of the Messiah is God."—1 Corinthians 11:3
>
> "As for husbands, love your wives, just as the Messiah loved the Messianic Community, indeed, gave himself up on its behalf, in order to set it apart for God, making it clean through immersion in the mikveh (immersion pool), so to speak, in order to present the Messianic Community to himself as a bride to be proud of, without a spot, wrinkle or any such thing, but holy and without defect. This is how husbands ought to love their wives —like their own bodies; for the man who loves his wife is loving himself. Why, no one ever hated his own flesh! On the contrary, he feeds it well and takes care of it, just as the Messiah does the Messianic Community, because we are parts of his Body. 'Therefore a man will leave his father and mother and remain with his wife, and the two will become one.' There is a profound truth hidden here, which I say concerns the Messiah and the Messianic Community."—Ephesians 5:25-32

From these two Scriptures, we see clearly the analogy of the Messiah as the Bridegroom and the Messianic Community (the

Body of Believers, Jews and Gentiles together) as the Bride. All of the members of the Messiah's global congregation make up His Bride. He then joins Himself in marriage to His Bride, and the two become one. As one being, no longer two separates, the Messiah becomes the head, since He is the husband, and the believers the body. Hence, each and every one of us makes up the Body of the Messiah, IF we are joined to the global congregation. This is a marriage relationship between the Body of Believers and the Messiah, not a casual acquaintance. Similarly, we can't be casually involved with the Body of Believers, or we'll be left behind when He comes for His Bride.

Yeshua was totally committed to doing God's will. His purpose on earth was to do the will of the Father. Hence, our purpose on earth is to do the will of the Father as well, since we are one with the Messiah. The Messiah is coming back for a Bride without a spot or wrinkle. Since, we know that He is perfect and holy, then we must allow Him to transform us so that we'll be perfect and holy when He returns, individually and collectively. Otherwise, we would cause the Messiah to be unequally yoked in His marriage to His Bride at the time of His return, thus making Him a hypocrite because He failed to fulfill His own commands to us through Sha'ul, not to be unequally yoked[297].

Our failure to commit ourselves to the local and global Body makes us adulterous in our marriage relationship to Yeshua. With such a wife, the Messiah will not unite Himself. Hence, all such so-called "believers" will not be counted among the Body of Believers called the Bride when the Messiah returns.[298] Remember, He's coming back for a congregation, not scattered individuals doing their own things. Such believers will be left for judgment with all those who had not believed, just as the Messiah warned the body of believers in Laodicea saying, "I know what you are doing: you are neither cold nor hot. How I wish you were either one or the other! So, because you are lukewarm, neither cold nor hot, I will vomit you out of my mouth!"[299]

CHAPTER 11
PUTTING FEET ON MY FAITH
-JAMES' TESTIMONY-

"Suppose a brother or sister is without clothes and daily food, and someone says to him, 'Shalom! Keep warm and eat hearty!' without giving him what he needs, what good does it do? Thus, faith by itself, unaccompanied by actions, is dead."—James 2:15-17

James is a minister of outreach and evangelism. God appointed him to ensure that the ministry in which he serves assists those in the community in need of food, housing, clothing or any social services. Though the ministry cannot always provide these things, he knows just where to refer individuals if they need additional assistance. He walks in this calling even outside of his ministry duties by visiting the sick and shut-in, sharing his testimony and proclaiming the Good News to everyone he meets. He is always ready to offer a word of encouragement to the disenfranchised and discouraged, and he helps people to stop looking at the problems in their situations and allow God to teach them something new through their suffering. All this he does with a smile on his face and an outstretched hand.

The press upon James to serve in outreach ministry is always strengthened by his memory of where God brought him from. Eighteen years ago, James was separated from his wife, abusing cocaine and alcohol, and chasing women. His entire life was centered around getting more, whether it was alcohol, cocaine or women. He used his people skills and pleasant smile to get what he wanted. He would strategically place himself in people's lives just so that he would be there when an opportunity presented itself for him to take advantage of their needs. He lied without hesitation and spent every waking moment feeding his addictions or planning ways to feed them later.

James finally reached a point when he realized he was no longer in control and hadn't been for a long time. One day he sat with a gun in his hand and cried out to Adonai, "I don't want to die, but I can't keep on living like this." Though his intention for that day had been to get high and then end his own life, Yeshua showed up and delivered him instantly. He took the taste for alcohol and cocaine out of James' mouth and his body. James no longer wanted to get high and walked away from the stash he had bought that day, but God wasn't done working on him.

James later became a part of a 12-step fellowship and got a sponsor who helped to guide him through the process of getting clean. While there, he realized that God had moved miraculously on his behalf. People often asked him how long he was in detox or how long he went for treatment. His answer was always, "I didn't go." He began to realize that everyone's experience with quitting had not been the same as his own. The Messiah delivered him instantly without the help of medical science. Now James is the last person who would ever put down treatment programs, he even refers people to them because they do work and many people need them to get clean and sober, but that hadn't been his experience.

God had directly intervened for him to save his life. That meant he must be special to God. The realization of God's personal love for him led him to want to find out more about His Deliverer. So, he would sneak off to a worship service or read books because he just had to be filled with new knowledge, but something was still missing.

The success of any 12-step fellowship in breaking addictive habits rests on relationship with God. Step 11 states, "We sought through prayer and meditation to improve our conscious contact with God as we understood Him, praying only for knowledge of His will for us and the power to carry that out."[300] While working this step, James' sponsor said to him, "How can you improve something you don't have?" That was what James was missing, conscious contact with God—a personal relationship.

Though James had stopped drinking and using, he still continued in the lifestyle that he was used to for four years after that day Yeshua delivered him from addiction. His lying, running the streets and lust for women left him jobless, homeless and penniless. It was at this low point in his life when he realized that ADONAI was drawing him. James had to move into a homeless shelter as a result of his actions. While there, he met a young lady he liked. She invited him to a worship service. Being who he was at the time, he wasn't thinking about worshipping, but wanted to get closer to her. However, God had a plan.

This was a worship service at which many ministries came together and the bishop over those ministries preached. As he preached about forgiveness, it spoke directly to James' feelings at the time about being betrayed by someone close to him. Even the example the bishop used seemed to come directly from James' life. As he closed out his sermon, he walked through the congregation and placed his hand on James' shoulder while he concluded the message.

Then the call to discipleship[301] was given, and the bishop said, "You need to give yourself to Christ right now if you haven't, because the next moment is not promised to you. You could leave this place, walk outside and be hit by a bus, and you would never make it into heaven." Though James remained in his seat, the Ruach HaKodesh kept pulling at his heart. After the service, he asked one of the ministers, who was new to ministry himself, how he could become a member of the body. The young man told him to come back next Sunday. "Come back next Sunday?" James exclaimed. "That man just said I need to come to Christ today 'cause I could get hit by a bus."

James gave his life to the Messiah that day and joined the ministry. As a result of his obedience to answering Yeshua's call to salvation and discipleship, he had an instantaneous spiritual change. He still has trouble describing it, but he felt lighter, like a load was lifted from him. He began the next day as a new man, committed to living a different lifestyle based upon his personal relationship with the Messiah.

James continued with that ministry for a while but began to feel that something was missing. He didn't always feel that he played an important role there or that the members really cared for him personally. When he missed services sometimes, no one would come to check on him or call him. He wasn't getting everything he felt he needed emotionally or spiritually. So, rather abruptly, James left the ministry and joined another, still looking for something he had not yet found. James ended up joining various ministries over the course of the years as his soul searched for a place where he would get all that he needed, even though he didn't know exactly what that was, and find his own place in the Body of the Messiah.

Some time later, a long-time friend of his and minister of God was called to build a new ministry. At the time, the two of them were in fellowship in the same congregation, yet God had called her to start a new congregation. Because James recognized the Messiah in this woman, and he had known her for quite some time, he felt a press in his spirit to go with her to start this new ministry. James became an integral part in the establishment of the congregation, but he still struggled for two years about God's purpose for his life and how to fulfill it.

For most of that time, Yeshua tugged on his heart about serving in the body as a minister. Though he wrestled with the call for a while, he eventually accepted it. Immediately after accepting the call, God began to put him in places where he was needed to minister to God's people—not just in the ministry, but outside of it as well. Since James surrendered his life to the Messiah, Yeshua has never left him nor forsaken him. His road has been long and hard, but full of God's grace, mercy and provisions.

James' testimony has been a tool for him to evangelize to lost souls, to demonstrate the love of the Messiah through reaching out and helping individuals, and to be an example to us all about how miraculously God can and will work in the lives of His people. Since being strategically positioned in the Body of the Messiah, God has used James even more effectively in ministry. James doesn't even look the same as he did before accepting his call. No matter where he goes, people recognize him as a minister of God due to the anointing on his life.

CONCLUSION
EXTENDED TRANSFORMING EXPERIENCES

"As for you, Shlomo (Solomon) my son, know the God of your father. Serve him wholeheartedly and with desire in your being; for ADONAI searches all hearts and understands all the inclinations of people's thoughts. If you seek him, he will let himself be found by you; but if you abandon him, he will reject you forever."

1 Chronicles 28:9

CHAPTER 12
EXTENDED TRANSFORMING EXPERIENCES

"To him Yeshua said, 'No one who puts his hand to the plow and keeps looking back is fit to serve in the Kingdom of God.'"—Luke 9:62

Have you ever had to put together a new piece of furniture or assemble a complicated toy for your child? Maybe you had to go to a place you've never been to and time was of the essence. In either scenario, it's always tempting to try to figure it out ourselves rather than reading the instructions, looking at the map or asking for help. Our pride wants to be able to say, "look ma, I did it all by myself." You'll note that I used a phrase most children use to declare their independence in accomplishing a task. When we want to declare independence in our accomplishments, we sound just like that, little children.

As parents, we want our children to be self-sufficient and capable. So, when they're able to do something new, we applaud them and give them praise. However, that statement, "look ma, I did it all by myself," is inherently flawed for a few reasons. It fails to recognize the hundreds of times mom and dad had to do it for the child, the training the parents gave the child, the support given to the child and even that the feat accomplished by the child was made possible by some provision from the parents (i.e. tying their shoes—mom and dad bought the shoes, using the potty—mom and dad bought the potty, getting dressed—mom and dad bought the clothes; you get the point).

The same is true in our relationships with our Father. We want so badly to say, "look God, I did it all by myself," but once we come into the knowledge of the Messiah, our loving Father won't allow us to do that. He knows that all such boasts are proud, and they'll keep us from truly worshipping Him, appreciating Him and developing into the people He created us to be. We can't do anything without Him; in order for us to really receive the power of God, we have to first recognize our dependency on Him.

Our example above of assembling the furniture or toy demonstrates for us the mindsets we often have when Adonai calls us to a new ministry for Him. We might accept the call eagerly (and that's a big might), but then we want to do it all alone, WITHOUT reading the instructions (in the Bible) or asking for help (in prayer). Our example of going to a new destination resembles our attitudes when Yeshua is taking us to a new level in Him; once again we don't want to read the map (the Bible) or ask for directions (in prayer). This despite the fact that we've never been there before and none of our requisite knowledge is going to help us find the new place because it's not like any place we've ever been. So, we delay our arrival time and often miss out on blessings that were waiting for us in a particular season of our lives.

Being called to a new ministry and going to a new level in the Messiah both necessitate transformation. Transformation is a process of changing from one form to another. Thus, we need to be transformed every time Yeshua wants to do something new with us so that our character will meet the challenge. When ADONAI brought our fathers (physical or spiritual) out of Egypt and into the Promised Land, His desire was to transform them from a nation of slaves into a nation of priests. They had been in bondage for 430 years and now they were expected to be warriors, stewards and examples of God's love to the world. That's quite a change. For this reason, the journey from Egypt to the land of Canaan doubled as a transforming experience for the children of Isra'el.

The trip from Egypt to Canaan could have taken the children of Isra'el 11 days. Instead it took 40 years. ADONAI had to extend their transformation to insure that they were ready to inherit the Promised Land when He sent them in to claim it. So, rather than going right in, they had to travel around a mountain in the desert for 40 years. During which time, some people and mindsets that were disobedient to God died and He was able to give birth to a new generation with a new perspective to take the Promised Land.

The transforming experience of the children of Isra'el coming out of Egypt was extended because of their disobedience, lack of trust, holding on to their old way of life in bondage, and complaining about God's method of deliverance. Much like the children of Isra'el in the desert, we prolong our own transforming experiences by trying to guide them ourselves. We haven't the knowledge or power to transform ourselves from slaves to sin into anointed servants of El 'Elyon (God Most High). Yet instead of surrendering to His will and ways, we fight Him all the way. (Don't feel bad, I think I'm the president of this "resist God's transformation" club.) Some transforming experiences are easier for us than others, but no matter which part of us He's trying to change, our response should always be the same.

Thus far, we've looked at the divine perfection of the transformation of a young Parush (Pharisee) named Sha'ul into a mighty emissary and servant of Messiah Yeshua. His transformation is an excellent example for us of what to do during every transforming experience we have with Yeshua. Failure to respond as Sha'ul responded will always delay our deliverance and drag out transformation in our lives. Sha'ul's transformation was immediate for a few reasons:

1. he accepted the Messiah's invitation to follow Him,
2. he reevaluated everything he believed,
3. he had a sincere desire to please God, and
4. he immediately turned away from his sins and adjusted his lifestyle.

Each one of us can experience transformation just as Sha'ul did. When we don't, it's because we're lacking in one of the four areas mentioned above. This is what I call an extended transforming experience. Often times, we're not changed in God's perfect timing because we don't accept the Messiah's invitation, we don't reevaluate what we believe, we don't sincerely desire to please God, or we don't turn away from our sins and adjust our lifestyles.

Accepting the Messiah's Invitation

In the 26th chapter of Acts, Sha'ul recounts his encounter with the Messiah as he stands trial before King Agrippa to defend his ministry as an emissary, because many had labeled him a troublemaker and lawbreaker. In verse 14, he recounts the first words the Messiah spoke to him, but a sentence is added that was not mentioned in chapter 9. It reads, "Sha'ul! Sha'ul! Why do you keep persecuting me? It's hard on you to be kicking against the ox-goads!" This expression of "kicking against the goads"[302] or "kicking against the prick"[303] refers to something similar to a cattle prod used on oxen. A cattle prod pokes the cattle to make them go in a certain direction. Similarly, God was poking Sha'ul to get him to go in God's direction for his life, but he was resisting God's guidance. Thus, Yeshua's statement to Sha'ul simply means 'stop fighting because you are only hurting yourself.' God had a plan for Sha'ul's life, and he needed to stop fighting against it.

When we hear of transforming experiences, we often hear of people who accepted the Messiah's invitation immediately, and then He miraculously changed their lives and sent them to work. We know that accepting invitations is not that simple, though. Satan doesn't know God's plan for each of us, so he operates off of what he hears and reads. It's not until an invitation becomes extended to us that the enemy begins to realize that God is planning to use us or elevate us in some way. Then we appear on the enemy's radar screen. If we accept Yeshua's invitation for next level transformation, we will have to be immersed in fire (which often falls under Satan's list of duties). However, we'll be protected by God, who will only allow the suffering and persecution to go so far. He said that He would not allow us to be tempted beyond what we can bear, and He will provide a way out, so that we can endure it.[304]

Conversely, we also have the choice of NOT accepting the Messiah's invitation for next level transformation. This, of course, is to our own detriment though. If we don't accept Yeshua's invitation, Satan knows about that too. He then identifies us as potential warriors in God's army and begins to form plans against us. As long as he thinks we're no threat to his dominion here on earth,[305] he won't vigorously attack us. But once we're identified as a potential threat, all bets are off and the enemy pulls out his big guns to take us out. The Messiah's instructions during our transforming experiences are often for our protection against the attacks of the enemy. However, if we refuse to accept the Messiah's invitation to go to the next level, we're left unprotected against the enemy's attacks, which, but the way, have been upgraded to the level we're SUPPOSED to be going to. Our rebellion and resultant sins open us up to more attacks from the adversary than ever before.

We'll look at two Scripture texts to give us a better understanding of this. Second Peter 2:20-22 reads, "Indeed, if they have once escaped the pollutions of the world through knowing our Lord and Deliverer, Yeshua the Messiah, and then have again become entangled and defeated by them, their latter condition has become worse than their former. It would have been better for them not to have known the Way of righteousness than, fully knowing, to turn from the holy command delivered to them. What has happened to them accords with the true proverb, 'A dog returns to its own vomit.' Yes, 'The pig washed itself, only to wallow in the mud!'"[306] Additionally, Matthew 12:43-45 reads, "When an unclean spirit comes out of a person, it travels through dry country seeking rest and does not find it. Then it says to itself, 'I will return to the house I left.' When it arrives, it finds the house standing empty, swept clean and put in order. Then it goes and takes with it seven other spirits more evil than itself, and they come and live there—so that in the end, the person is worse off than he was before. This is how it will be for this wicked generation."

God doesn't want us to suffer, even at our own hands, which is why Yeshua said to Sha'ul, "It's hard on you to be kicking against the ox-goads!" There is no middle road with Yeshua. Refusing to serve the Messiah means we're serving Satan[307] and refusing to go deeper in our relationship with the Messiah so that He can take us higher is to remain stagnant, which eventually leads to a slow spiritual death. Once Satan realizes that God wants to give us more power and anointing, all he wants to do is destroy us in our sin before we get another chance to serve Yeshua wholeheartedly. For this reason, people who have a personal encounter with Yeshua but refuse to accept His invitation at that time end up on a downward spiral of sin leading to death. They get into strongholds, in which they continue to live in a manner that's contrary to God, but they feel helpless to control themselves.[308] Yet in the will of God, no weapon made will prevail against us.[309]

Reevaluating Our Beliefs

Earlier in Chapter 26 of Acts, Sha'ul shares with King Agrippa the reason the children of Isra'el are persecuting him. Sha'ul shares that the Jews all know that he lived as a Parush (Pharisee), the strictest sect of their religion. He then states, "How ironic it is that I stand on trial here because of my hope in the promise made to our fathers! It is the fulfillment of this very promise that our twelve tribes hope to attain, as they resolutely carry on their acts of worship night and day; yet it is in connection with this hope, your Majesty, that I am being accused by Jews!"[310]

He goes on to say, "I used to think it was my duty to do all I could to combat the name of Yeshua from Natzeret."[311] Sha'ul tells us here that he too was committed to persecuting the believers because he was convinced that it was right. Additionally, he shares that his accusers "resolutely carry on their acts of worship night and day." These two statements show that though they were misdirected, the Jews persecuting Sha'ul and young Sha'ul himself, had a strong desire to please God. However, without the knowledge of the Messiah to lead them, they were interpreting the Scriptures and God's will incorrectly.

Yeshua said He is the Way, the Truth and the Life.[312] Hence, to know Him is to know the Truth; not to know Him is not to know the Truth. Before we come into the knowledge of the Messiah, we live deluded lives. Our personal encounters with Him should pull away layers of delusion from our minds, piece by piece. That's why we must accept every invitation and then reevaluate everything we think we know. We encounter problems when we don't allow the knowledge of the Messiah to challenge everything we believe. We must become fools for Him, so that He can make us wise.[313]

If we insist upon holding onto our beliefs after an encounter with Yeshua, we'll extend our transforming experience and bring unnecessary pain and suffering upon ourselves and those around us. God will then be forced to allow things to occur that will challenge our beliefs, so much so that we'll either surrender our beliefs to God so that He might teach us or we'll leave the Way and stop serving Him altogether. Sha'ul surrendered his beliefs. He allowed the knowledge of the Messiah to change his view of the Scriptures, the Good News and his own purpose in life. Doing this will turn our whole world upside down again and again, but that's what it's supposed to do. We were on a road to death and destruction, but Yeshua came to place us on the road to eternal life. And the two roads are miles apart. Getting there takes a lifetime.

Desire to Please God

As we continue in the text of Acts chapter 26, Sha'ul begins to share the things he did while dedicated to opposing the name of Yeshua. The second part of verse 10 through verse 11 reads, "After receiving authority from the head cohanim (chief priests), I myself threw many of God's people in prison; when they were put to death, I cast my vote against them. Often, I went from one synagogue to another, punishing them and trying to make them blaspheme; and in my wild fury against them, I even went so far as to persecute them in cities outside the country." Just as God did with Sha'ul, He can take the passion and energy that we dedicated to wrong living and incorrect religious ideals and apply it to our lives in the Messiah. Sha'ul the emissary was just as committed to carrying out his mission as was Sha'ul the Parush (Pharisee). Before his transformation, he was willing to kill for God. After his transformation, he was willing to die for Him.

Transformation changes our direction and our perspectives. However, we must be just as committed to the

Messiah after the transformation as we were to sin and delusion before the transformation. At some point during our transformation, we must receive from the Ruach that what we are being delivered from is in fact sin. It may be cowardice, complacency, false doctrine or even a form of pride (anything that focuses on us) that we wouldn't previously consider pride. Many people have extended transforming experiences because they don't sincerely desire to please God. Instead of transferring all of their drive and passion for self-fulfillment into a drive and passion for God, they attempt to hold on to worldly concepts, religious ideals, sinful living or self-will while serving God. We can't serve two masters,[314] and we can't take that stuff to the next level with us.

Even serving in a ministry is not a replacement for sincerely serving God. We must serve Him His way! Acts of tzedakah (righteousness) and the work of ministry cannot save us from Sh'ol (the place of the dead). When done with an impure heart and the wrong motives, they'll still pull us away from the Messiah. Instead, we should love ADONAI with all our hearts and demonstrate our love through our obedience. Our refusal to choose life over death will send us straight to Sh'ol, even in the Body of Believers. Yeshua says, "Any tree that does not produce good fruit is cut down and thrown in the fire! So, you will recognize them by their fruit. Not everyone who says to me, 'Lord, Lord!' will enter the Kingdom of Heaven, only those who do what my Father in heaven wants. On that Day, many will say to me, 'Lord, Lord! Didn't we prophesy in your name? Didn't we expel demons in your name? Didn't we perform many miracles in your name?' Then I will tell them to their faces, 'I never knew you! Get away from me, you workers of lawlessness!'"[315] And who are the workers of lawlessness? . . . Those who reject the Word of God, which is Law.

Turning Away from Sin and Making Lifestyle Adjustments

As Sha'ul continues in his defense, he goes on to share the vision of the Messiah. Then in verses 19 and 20 he states, "So, King Agrippa, I did not disobey the vision from heaven! On the contrary, I announced first in Damascus, then in

Yerushalayim and throughout Y'hudah (Judea), and also to the Goyim (Gentiles), that they should turn from their sins to God and then do deeds consistent with that repentance." Sha'ul could proclaim that message of repentance because that was also what he did. Yeshua's appearance to him on the road to Damascus allowed him to see himself as he was: a blaspheming, violent, arrogant man who used religion as an excuse to sin directly against God.[316] He didn't try to justify his sin; he acknowledged what it was.

Turning away from sins for him, as we have explored before, was to work for the Son of God, whom he had been working against. God had to purge him of his wrath and arrogance in order to use him effectively in ministry. Sha'ul never raised a hand to anyone again even though he himself was beaten, stoned, cursed, and much more. There's no way Sha'ul could have suffered as the Messiah suffered and continued to be an arrogant, violent man. Retaliation would have always been on his mind. Instead of being imprisoned for proclaiming the Good News, he would have been imprisoned for starting fights or murdering someone who persecuted him.[317] That would have brought no glory to God.

In his obedience to the vision, Sha'ul also adjusted his lifestyle. He began immediately to live as a follower of the Messiah. He laid down his life as a Parush (Pharisee). In fact, he didn't even report back to the high priest. He just allowed the Ruach HaKodesh to transform him into a believer. His friends changed immediately; he began to associate with other believers. He didn't go back to Yerushalayim to try to hang out with his buddies among the P'rushim (Pharisees) who were still persecuting believers. Rather, he presented himself to the very people he had been persecuting, because he knew that he needed to be in fellowship with them for the mission to be completed. He didn't allow shame or guilt to keep him from staying with the believers in Damascus. He didn't even allow shame or guilt to keep him from going to the disciples in Yerushalayim.[318] Sha'ul knew that God would make a way. His allegiance was to the Messiah first, and every other decision he made was directed by that allegiance.

Beloved, when we have an encounter with Yeshua, we must heed his instructions for repentance and adjust our lifestyles accordingly. This completes the transforming experience. Remember, transformation means to be changed. We can't undergo changes in our hearts, minds and spirits, without making some significant changes to our behaviors and physical environments. The change of heart, mind and spirit will not last if we don't turn away from our sins and make the necessary lifestyle adjustments.

This is true for everyone who has ever and will ever experience a transformation into the image of the Messiah. During my first transforming experience, I had to stop fornicating, change the type of clothes I wore, and even stop watching certain programs on TV because they brought those thoughts back into my mind and provided me with arguments to justify fornication. Regina had to stay away from her child's father, read the Word of God and fellowship with the women at her church who could continue to minister to her situation. James had to stop lying, stop manipulating people, and stay in fellowship with a body of believers.

Remaining in fellowship with believers and reading the Bible are essential elements for any transforming experience, but there are always specific things each believer should do to ensure that he doesn't find himself in the same situation again. Turning away from our sins and making lifestyle adjustments connect us to our new life and a new way of living. They also disconnect us from our old life and old way of living. We can't walk into the light and bring the darkness with us, for darkness and light have no fellowship with each other.[319] You're going to have to let go of some people, places and things, for your own good. What we used to do, where we used to do it and with whom we used to do it will always be a temptation for us, even after we've been delivered.

Our Biblical example, Sha'ul, had to change his surroundings too. It's not a coincidence that he was sent to proclaim the Good News to the Gentiles. In verse 30 of chapter 9, Sha'ul is sent out of Yerushalayim to another country. He didn't remain in familiar territory long. He was now an enemy to those with whom he had worked. This will be true for you as well. Many of your old friends won't like you and accept you, even those who are believers. Your transformation into the likeness of the Messiah will be an affront to them personally and turn you into the target for their guilt, frustrations and anger. Turning from sin and making lifestyle adjustments go hand-in-hand. Together, they serve many vital roles in our transformations, which make them necessary parts of our experience with the Messiah. We can't overlook their importance if we desire lasting change.

The Extended Transforming Experience of the Body of the Messiah

The global Body of the Messiah has had an extended transforming experience as well. Yeshua received all authority in heaven and on earth, and then empowered believers to make disciples of all nations through that authority.[320] During the time shortly after His resurrection, many Jews and Gentiles received the Good News of salvation with joy. However, many of the Gentiles did not reevaluate everything they believed and thus opened the door first for syncretism, then for outright rebellion.

Syncretism is when two religions are mixed together forming a new hybrid filled with inconsistencies, as it is based on opposing doctrines. Proud and undelivered Gentile believers incorporated paganism into belief in the Messiah. The most noticeable sign of this was the First Council of Nicea in 325 A.D. Though its goals were to settle disputes between groups of believers by creating one doctrine for all, a commitment to syncretism caused the council to exclude all Jews from the Body of Believers and turn away from the Bible (because it is a distinctly Jewish book), thrusting the Body into an extended transforming experience.

So, from the 4th to the 16th century, the Body of the Messiah wandered in the desert in complete rebellion toward God. The Ruach HaKodesh was no longer leading those who professed faith in the Messiah because the branches were disconnected from their roots.[321] Hence, leaders in the Church devised ways to try and fulfill the Great Commission through their flesh. This accounts for such atrocities as the Crusades, the Spanish Inquisition and many others during this time period.

In God's great mercy, He began to carry the Body of Believers through a series of stages in order to return it to His original intent. Because we had walked away from Him, we have to backtrack in order to return to Him. Hence, the order of the stages He used (and is using) to draw us back to the Messiah is exactly opposite of the order in which He desires for us to operate when reclaiming territory for Him. As you will recall from chapter 10 of this book and Ephesians 4:11, the Messiah first sends the emissaries (apostles), then the prophets, proclaimers of the Good News (evangelists), shepherds (pastors) and teachers when He wants to reclaim territory for Himself. So, as He began to return us to Himself, the Body first went through the Teaching Age, then the Pastoral Age, the Evangelistic Age, the Prophetic Age and now we are in the Apostolic Age, which ushers in the return of Messiah.

The Teaching Age

As the Body started to backtrack its way to the Messiah, the Teaching Age began. This age is characterized by the Protestant Reformation of the 16th century in which believers broke away from the Roman Catholic Church. The Protestant Reformers went back to the Bible and the Good News of Yeshua through the doctrines of "sola scriptura" and "sola fide." "Sola scriptura" asserts that the Bible—as God's written Word—is self-authenticating, clear to Spirit-led readers, its own interpreter ("Scripture interprets Scripture"), and sufficient of itself to be the only source of doctrine for believers in Yeshua. "Sola fide" asserts that only by faith in God's grace are we forgiven our sins.

You will recall that the Teacher among the five-fold ministers is the one who checks everything done in the Body by the Bible. Hence, the Protestant Reformers, like Martin Luther, were the first believers since the Church's departure in 325 A.D. to rise up as five-fold teachers. They themselves were still in need of much deliverance, after having been separated from the root for so long, which accounts for the many errors they made. However, they were used by God as five-fold teachers in many ways including translating the Bible into various languages to get it into the hands of lay members of the Body.

The Pastoral Age

The next age to come was, of course, the Pastoral Age out of which arose various denominations. At this point in history, believers sought to form systems in which God's sheep could be discipled around specific Biblical doctrine. After the destruction of Yerushalayim in 70 A.D., the center of the Body of the Messiah was moved to Rome. When the Eastern Orthodox Church separated itself in the 11th century, its center became Constantinople, now Istanbul, Turkey. The Protestant churches, however, never created a new center after breaking away from Rome. Without five-fold emissaries and a center for the Body, five-fold shepherds began to form groups throughout the world that became our modern denominations.

Just as each individual believer has a call and mission from the Messiah, so does each ministry. Each ministry receives specific revelation and guidance in order to be all the Messiah would have it to be within the global Body. Hence, founders of denominations during the Pastoral Age built upon the specific revelation of Scripture and mission they received from the Messiah. In this way, they formed whole denominations rather than just churches from just after the Protestant Reformation until well into the 20th century. In the Apostolic Age, the revelation and mission of each denomination is coming together to make the Body of the Messiah full and complete, lacking nothing.

The Evangelistic Age

The third age is easily identified by most believers; it is the Evangelistic Age. During this age, believers pulled away from the rituals of religion into experiences of salvation. The need for God's grace as demonstrated through the Messiah's sacrifice became the main focus of revivals and even the birth of many movements and new ministries. The Evangelistic Age began with Lutheran churches in Europe in the 16th century just after the Protestant Reformation, then with the Puritans in the Church of England in the 17th century, and later the First and Second Great Awakenings in the United States in the 1730s through the 1740s and the 1800s through the 1830s respectively. The Third Great Awakening from the 1850s to the 1900s then paved the way for the Worldwide Missions Movement.

The Evangelistic Age took the focus off of churches (which began in the Pastoral Age) and placed it on the individual believer. This age also led to world missions in the Name of Jesus alone and even the birth of ministries with the mission of world evangelism, rather than church formation (as in the Pastoral Age). Prior to this age, the only ministries that were born within the Body were new church congregations. As the Evangelistic Age reaches full maturity, we see that believers have brought more people into faith in the Messiah in the past 200 years than in the entire history of the Body of Believers since its early formation documented in the Book of Acts. We are now measurably close to fulfilling the Great Commission, and this is due only to the fact that five-fold evangelists have been commissioned to proclaim the Good News all over the world.

The Prophetic and Apostolic Ages

The Body of Believers then went into the fourth age, the Prophetic Age. You will recall that God uses prophets to illuminate the direction in which He is taking the global Body, to reveal new strategies in defeating spiritual wickedness in high places, to predict the coming moves of God, and to uncover sinful trends in the Body. Most emphasis among believers has been on contemporary prophets, like Chuck Pierce, who illuminate the direction in which God is taking the Body and predict the coming moves of God, such as began with the Latter Rain Movement in the 1950s. However, the Prophetic Age began to come into its maturity as prophets like Rabbi Jonathan Cahn began boldly proclaiming from every corner of the earth the sins of believers and unbelievers, particularly those in leadership positions. This conviction paves the way for the apostolic anointing to address strongholds.

The Prophetic Age was set strategically by El Shaddai (God Almighty) to prepare the world for the Apostolic Age, the culmination of which will be the return of the Chief Apostle,[322] Yeshua the Messiah, to the earth. The Prophetic Age is sweeping over the earth with an Elijah anointing,[323] such as was on Yochanan the Immerser (John the Baptist), to prepare the world for the Apostolic Age in which believers advance the Kingdom of God by force.[324] We began to see the beginning of the Apostolic Age as leaders and ministries in the Body shifted their focus onto the Kingdom, with ministries even changing their names to include "Kingdom" in the title. The full power of the apostolic anointing was not released, however, until after the Prophetic Age reached maturity, as characterized by public conviction of national and religious leaders through prophets (without apology), unimaginable alliances within the global Body, and an influx of signs and wonders. All of this is preparation for Messiah's Millennial Reign.

We will not see the fullness of the signs and wonders until well into the Apostolic Age, though. Because emissaries tear down spiritual strongholds, the resurgence of the apostolic commission will free whole nations from spiritual and political oppression, idolatry, famine and plagues in very short periods of time. Yeshua said that we would do greater works than He.[325] The release of the apostolic anointing will finally make this possible. The anointing and the wonders that follow are for the express purpose of advancing the Kingdom of God in preparation for the Messiah's return.

The return of the full apostolic anointing will so alarm the Adversary, that during the Apostolic Age he will commission his anti-Messiah, a false apostle. The spirit of anti-Messiah is already at work in the earth. The spirit of false prophecy that prepares the way before anti-Messiah has begun to set the stage through Islam, spiritualism and the "one-world religion" movement we see bombarding society. Many end times movements toward syncretism, like Chrislam (Christianity and

Islam), also desensitize the world population to this type of false prophecy.

When God moves powerfully, the enemy always tries to copy the moves of God, but his counterstrategies are based on lies and moral impurity. The Prophetic and Apostolic Ages prepare believers to discern the difference between the moves of God and the moves of the Adversary in the world. However, our individual transforming experiences and the collective transformation of the Body of the Messiah (restoring order through the regrafting of the children of Isra'el into the Body and restoring power and authority through the resurgence of five-fold ministry) will insure that believers are mature and prepared for the anti-Messiah's deception and the Messiah's return. In Matthew 24:24, Yeshua says that false messiahs and false prophets will TRY to deceive even the elect. The transformation of the Body of the Messiah and all of its parts will make this impossible for true believers.

The Choice

At this point in your life, God is bringing many things before you to show you that you must make a choice between life and death. If you have not yet received the Messiah as your Savior, that is the choice He is calling you to make. If, however, you have received Him, then you must discern the next-level transformation through which He wants to take you and choose His way in His Word over that which has been comfortable for you in your walk with Him thus far. Don't disregard the teachings and sermons that speak directly into your situation, the phone calls you receive that convict you of sin, the closeness you're feeling to the Messiah, the discomfort you now feel when you do things you have always done, or the conviction you have received while reading this book. These are all signs that God is extending an invitation to you. When the invitation comes, in whatever form it may come, accept what God offers for the building of His Kingdom and your transformation into the image of the Messiah.

Yeshua speaks about the invitation in a parable to his disciples. You can find it in Matthew 22:1-14. In this parable, honorable people had been invited to the wedding banquet of the king's son but refused to attend. So, the king sent the invitation to others, those without honor, and many accepted. However, one person was not wearing wedding clothes, so he was thrown out of the banquet. Those who accepted the invitation are believers. Yet, we see from the man who was thrown out that believers must continue to choose the right way in order to STAY in the Kingdom. We must continue to accept the invitations of the Messiah to transform us into His image and make us into the righteousness of God.[326] The fellow without the wedding clothes represents anyone who accepts the Messiah's invitation to salvation, but does not accept the righteousness the Messiah offers through transformation, which is necessary to enter God's Kingdom.[327] For the Word says, "For this reason the wicked won't stand up to the judgment, nor will sinners at the gathering of the righteous."[328]

We can reject the Messiah in various ways, as described earlier in this chapter. However, any rejection of the Messiah will cause Him to reject us when we desire to enter God's Kingdom.[329] Hebrews 3:12-19 explains well the consequences of rejecting Yeshua and His righteousness. It reads,

> "Watch out, brothers, so that there will not be in any one of you an evil heart lacking trust, which could lead you to apostatize from the living God! Instead, keep exhorting each other every day, as long as it is called Today, so that none of you will become hardened by the deceit of sin. For we have become sharers in the Messiah, provided, however, that we hold firmly to the conviction we began with, right through until the goal is reached. Now where it says, 'Today, if you hear God's voice, don't harden your hearts, as you did in the Bitter Quarrel,' who were the people who, after they heard, quarreled so bitterly? All those whom Moshe (Moses) brought out of Egypt. And with whom was God disgusted for forty years? Those who sinned—yes, they fell dead in the Wilderness! And to whom was it that he swore that they would not enter his rest? Those

who were disobedient. So we see that they were unable to enter because of lack of trust."

"His rest," as the writer refers to it, is Shabbat (Sabbath) rest in the Kingdom of God.[330] We will have a place in God's Kingdom if we just accept, and continue to accept, the invitations of His Son.

"Here, I'm standing at the door, knocking. If someone hears my voice and opens the door, I will come in to him and eat with him, and he will eat with me. I will let him who wins the victory sit with me on my throne, just as I myself also won the victory and sat down with my Father on his throne. Those who have ears, let them hear what the Spirit is saying to the Messianic communities."

--Revelation 3:20-22

END NOTES

[1] See Isaiah 43:1 and Song of Solomon 6:3
[2] See Romans 6:23
[3] See John 10:10
[4] See 2 Corinthians 3:18 and Philippians 3:10-16
[5] See Romans 8:9-17 and Revelation 21:1-8
[6] See Colossians 1:19 & 2:9-10 and Ephesians 1:22-23
[7] See Ephesians 3:16-19 & 4:7-13
[8] See Ephesians 5:25-32
[9] See Matthew 3:4
[10] See Matthew 3:13-17
[11] See John 3:22-36
[12] Matthew 9:13
[13] Matthew 9:12
[14] Luke 7:41-48
[15] Romans 3:23
[16] See Leviticus 17:11 and Hebrews 9:22
[17] Philippians 2:12 (NIV)
[18] James 2:18-19, but please read the entire book of James regarding living like the Messiah.
[19] Joshua 24:15
[20] See Romans chapter 6 and Luke 11:23
[21] See Ephesians chapter 4
[22] I suggest reading all of Romans chapter 11.
[23] The P'rushim (Pharisees) were religious leaders in Yeshua's time. See Matthew 23:1-36 (also 3:7-12, 5:20, 9:11-12, 9:32-34, 15:1-20, 16:1-12 & 22:15-22) and Luke 18:11-14 for descriptions of the P'rushim (Pharisees).
[24] See Romans 9:1-5
[25] See Acts 6:8
[26] See Isaiah 55:8 and 1 Corinthians 1:18-25
[27] See Acts 9:1-2 and John 16:2
[28] See Joshua chapter 7
[29] See 1 Timothy 1:13; the writer of the letters to Timothy is the emissary Sha'ul (Apostle Paul), who is the young Parush (Pharisee) Sha'ul after his transforming experience.
[30] Who is Yeshua, see John 8:12
[31] See Romans 6:23
[32] John 10:10
[33] Romans 8:7
[34] See Malachi 3:6 and Hebrews 13:8
[35] See Matthew 18:14
[36] See Revelations 12:3-12 for a specific description of Satan being cast out. See also Isaiah 14:12-15 and Ezekiel 28:12-19 for analogous descriptions of Satan being cast from heaven.
[37] See Genesis Chapter 3 and Romans 5:12-21
[38] See Isaiah 59:2, Psalms 51:5 and Romans 7:18-25
[39] See Romans 5:6-21

[40] See Acts 26:5
[41] See Acts 22:3
[42] See Genesis 1:30 and Ezekiel 37:9-10
[43] See Luke 11:34-36, James 3:5-12
[44] See 2 Timothy 3:5
[45] See Luke 16:19-31, especially verse 31. Yeshua rose from the dead, and many still do not believe and turn from their sins.
[46] See also James 1:22-25
[47] See John 10:10
[48] See 1 Timothy 1:13-16
[49] See Galatians 4:1-3
[50] See Galatians 4:4-7
[51] See Joshua 5:12
[52] See Matthew 7:15-20, but read that whole chapter to understand more about bearing fruit
[53] See 1 Samuel 15:22-23
[54] See Matthew 13:1-23, especially verse 19, and Matthew 16:22-23
[55] See Matthew 12:43-45 and John 5:1-14
[56] See Acts 4:19
[57] "Deliver us from evil" appears in Adonai's Prayer for a very important reason. See Matthew 6:13 and Luke 11:4.
[58] See Deuteronomy 6:13, Joshua 24:14-15, Psalms 34, 112, & 128, Luke 12:4-12, and Revelation 14:6-7
[59] See Psalms 27, 37 & 139 and Hebrews 13:5-6
[60] See Psalms 37:4 and the entire book of Song of Solomon
[61] See Joshua 24:15
[62] See Acts 5:1-11
[63] See Acts 9:36-41
[64] See Acts 5:12-16
[65] See Romans 12:3-8
[66] See 2 Corinthians 5;18
[67] See Romans 8:34
[68] See 1 Corinthians 10:13
[69] See Ezekiel 1:28, Exodus 3:6 and Isaiah 6:5
[70] See Genesis 6:6, 1 Samuel 15:35, Isaiah 63:10, and Ephesians 4:30
[71] Isaiah 53:5, but read all of Isaiah 53 for more about Yeshua as the Suffering Servant.
[72] See Ephesians 5:25-32
[73] See 2 Samuel chapter 11
[74] See 2 Samuel 12:1-14 for the message of rebuke God sent to David. The story of his affair with Bat-Sheva (Bathsheba) is in the preceding chapter.
[75] Psalm 51:4
[76] See Romans 8:1 and John 8:3-11
[77] See Romans 8:28 and Genesis 50:20
[78] Ezekiel 18:30-32
[79] Luke 7:47

[80] See John 14:15 & 15:10, 1 John 2:5 & 5:1-2. The following Scriptures stress the importance of obedience: James 1:22-25, Matthew 19:17 & 28:20, Luke 11:28, John 17:6, Romans 2:13, Hebrews 5:8-9, 1 Peter 1:22, and 1 John 3:24.

[81] See James 1:2-4

[82] See Deuteronomy 32:21 and Romans 10:16-11:32

[83] See 2 Samuel 23:39 and 1 Chronicles 11:41. Uriyah is listed there as one of the warrior-heroes. Read 2 Samuel 23:8-23 and 1 Chronicles 11:10-25 to get a better understanding of David's warrior-heroes.

[84] See Romans 7:24-8:2

[85] See Hebrews 9:11-28

[86] See 2 Corinthians 7:9-10

[87] See Romans 12:1-2

[88] Penance is any act of reparation or self-punishment done in repentance for a sin.

[89] See Matthew 17:21. Begin reading at verse 14 for full understanding. See also Matthew 4:1-4 & 26:41.

[90] See 1 John 1:9-10, Psalms 38:18 and Leviticus 26:40-42

[91] See James 5:16, Acts 19:18 & Proverbs 28:13

[92] Read Romans chapter 7:14-25 to understand this a little better.

[93] See James 4:7-11

[94] See Acts 9:21 & 9:26

[95] See John 14:16-17, Acts 15:7-8 and Romans 8:9-11

[96] See Genesis chapter 3 and Romans 6:12-21

[97] See Hebrews 9:15

[98] See John 10:10

[99] See Galatians 3:1-5

[100] See 1 Timothy 1:15-20

[101] Read 1 Corinthians chapters 1 & 2, especially 2:16

[102] See James 4:7 and 1 Peter 5:5-10

[103] See Romans 3:25 & 5:9, Ephesians 1:7, 1 Peter 1:18-19, 1 John 1:7 and Revelation 1:5, 5:9-10 & 7:14

[104] See James 1:2-8

[105] See Leviticus 27:30-33, Nehemiah 10:37-38, Malachi 3:6-12, and 2 Corinthians 9:5-15

[106] See John 15:5-17, Luke 3:8-9 & 6:43-45, and Colossians 1:9-12. See also Isaiah 5:1-7 for a wonderful prophetic metaphor about God looking for good fruit from His people.

[107] See Proverbs Ch. 7, Song of Solomon 8:4 & 8-12, 1 Corinthians 6:13-20, and 1 Thessalonians 4:3-5

[108] See Ecclesiastes 5:5 NIV

[109] See Isaiah 54:5

[110] To minister simply means to serve; see 2 Timothy 4:2-5 and 1 Peter 4:10-11.

[111] To prophesy is to proclaim the Word of God as received directly from the Voice and Spirit of God. See Isaiah 6:1-13, Jeremiah 1:4-19, Ezekiel 2:1-3:11 and Amos 7:12-17.

[112] See Acts chapter 2 for more about the Ruach HaKodesh (Holy Spirit) coming upon God's people. When you accept Yeshua as the Messiah, the Ruach HaKodesh (Holy Spirit) is your guarantee that He is saving you from death; see 2 Corinthians 1:21-22 and Ephesians 1:13-14 for the guarantee.

[113] See Mark 6:7-13 and Isaiah 6:8-13

[114] An apostle is "a sent forth one", one sent by God with a specific message. My message is "Messiah is coming! Get ready!" This is the focus of everything I do in ministry. See Ephesians 4:11-16. See also 1 Corinthians chapters 3 & 9.

[115] See Joshua 4:1-7

[116] See Matthew 3:13-17 and Luke 12:49-50

[117] See Matthew 16:24, Luke 9:23, John 8:12 & 12:26, 1 Corinthians 11:1-3 and 1 Peter 2:21

[118] See Matthew 12:1-14 & 23:23-28, Mark 3:1-6 & 7:1-23, Luke 6:6-11, 13:10-17 & 14:1-6

[119] See John 5:30 & 8:28-29, Matthew 26:39-42 and Mark 14:36

[120] See Matthew 3:11

[121] See Matthew 3:13-17

[122] See Proverbs 15:8 and 15:29

[123] 1 Samuel 16:7b

[124] See John 14:16-17, 14:26 and 16:7-15 for Messiah's promise to the disciples that He would send them the Holy Spirit. Then read Acts chapter 2, which depicts the day that promise was fulfilled.

[125] See Acts 1:1-11

[126] See John 14:26

[127] See John 16:13-15 & 2 Peter 1:21

[128] See John 14:26

[129] See Acts 11:19-18 and 2 Thessalonians 2:13

[130] See John 16:13, Acts 11:12 & 16:6

[131] See Acts 1:8 & 2:4

[132] See Romans 8:26-27 & Jude 1:20

[133] See Romans 8:16, 2 Corinthians 5:5 and John 15:26-27

[134] See John 14:6-7

[135] See Acts 1:8

[136] See Matthew 3:16

[137] See Matthew 4:1-17

[138] See Acts 8:15-17

[139] Acts 18:24-28

[140] See Matthew 28:19-20 and John 16:5-15

[141] See John 1:1-2 and Revelation 19:13

[142] See Matthew 11:27, John 6:44-47, 14:6-24 & especially 15:1-17

[143] Matthew 5:44

[144] Read Romans 12:1-3 and 1 Corinthians chapter 2, in that order, to understand the transformation of our minds.

[145] Our process of refining as likened to silver is also addressed in Proverbs 25:4-5 and Isaiah 1:25

[146] See Genesis 29:34

[147] See Genesis 32:28

[148] See Numbers 3:5-13

[149] 1 Peter 2:5

[150] 1 Peter 2:9-10

[151] See Revelation 7:9-17
[152] See Revelation 20:4-6
[153] See Job 1:8
[154] Job 23:10
[155] See Revelation 12:9-10, Zechariah 3:1 and Job 1:6-11
[156] See Jeremiah 22:21-23
[157] James 1:2-4
[158] See Hebrews 10:12-18 and Philippians 3:12-14
[159] See Jeremiah 10:23-24, Luke 12:15-48, Colossians 1:9-14, 1 Timothy 4:8 & 6:12-16
[160] See 1 Corinthians 15:42-58 & 13:8-12, and Romans 8:10-23
[161] See 2 Corinthians 5:1-10
[162] See Ephesians 6:10-18 and 2 Corinthians 10:3-6
[163] See Romans chapter 6, 7:4-6 & 8:16-18
[164] See Hebrews 12:14
[165] See Matthew 5:17-20 and Luke 16:16-17
[166] See Hebrews 10:1, but read the whole chapter for more on this subject.
[167] See Romans 7:4-14
[168] Matthew 12:29
[169] See Daniel 2:19-23 and Matthew 11:25-26
[170] See Genesis 12:7-8, 13:18, and 26:15
[171] See Genesis 11:5-9
[172] Romans 14:23
[173] See also Proverbs 19:18
[174] Hebrews 12:5-8
[175] Hebrews 12:9-10
[176] Hebrews 12:11
[177] See Romans 8:28-39
[178] Isaiah 39:8
[179] Matthew 5:10-12
[180] See Acts 1:4 & 2:1-4
[181] See Matthew 4:1-11
[182] Matthew 7:13-14
[183] See Mark 8:34 & 10:35-40
[184] See Romans 5:1-5, Philippians 3:10-11, 2 Timothy 1:8, and 1 Peter 4:12-19
[185] See Romans 8:17-18
[186] See Genesis 2:29-30
[187] See Romans 6:6-7
[188] See John 3:1-21 and 1 Peter 1:13-25
[189] See Galatians 5:25 and Matthew 26:41
[190] See Jeremiah 4:3-4 and Hosea 10:11-13
[191] See Mark 4:1-32
[192] James 3:9-12
[193] See 1 Samuel 16:7 and 1 Chronicles 28:9

[194] See 1 Corinthians 3:10-17 and Philippians 1:6
[195] See Matthew 4:4
[196] See Luke 1:80 and John 6:63
[197] See John 14:16-26
[198] See Romans 7:14-25
[199] See James 1:13-15 and Romans 8:5-8
[200] See 2 Peter 1:2-9 and 1 Timothy 4:7-8
[201] See Romans 12:1-2, Ephesians 4:20-24 and Colossians 3:1-4
[202] See Hebrews 4:12, 2 Timothy 3:16-17 and Psalms 119
[203] See 1 Thessalonians 2:13
[204] See James 1:5-8
[205] See 1 Corinthians 3:10-20
[206] See Matthew 16:24
[207] See 1 Thessalonians 5:4-10, 1 John 1:5-10 & 2:9-11
[208] See Matthew 6:22-23
[209] See Matthew 16:1-4
[210] John 4:24 NIV
[211] See Matthew 8:28-31, Mark 1:34 & 5:2-13, and Luke 4:33-36
[212] See 1 Corinthians 2:16, but read verses 6-16 and 2 Corinthians 4:18-5:10
[213] See 1 Corinthians 1:17-31 and continue reading through all of chapter 2 as well.
[214] See 1 Corinthians 2:6-16
[215] "Akhor" means trouble.
[216] See Exodus 20:14, Leviticus 20:10, Matthew 5:27-30, and Hebrews 13:4
[217] See Acts 2:1-12, 1 Corinthians 12:10 & 13:1 & Ch. 14
[218] See 1 Corinthians 2:9-16 & 12:10 and 2 Corinthians 10:4-5
[219] See Acts 8:18-19, 1 Timothy 4:14 & 5:22, and 2 Timothy 1:6
[220] See Genesis 3:15 and Luke 10:18-19
[221] See Matthew 28:19-20a
[222] See John 15:14-15
[223] See Hebrews 2:10-11, John 1:12-13, Romans 8:15-16 and 1 John 3:1-2
[224] See Acts 1:8 and Matthew 24:13-14
[225] See Romans 8:17
[226] See Romans 10:16-21
[227] See Romans 11:25-26
[228] See Isaiah 52:13-15
[229] See also Isaiah 51:11
[230] See Isaiah 54:5
[231] See Isaiah 54:7-8
[232] See Isaiah 54:11-13
[233] See Isaiah 54:16-17
[234] See 2 Corinthians 5:17-19
[235] John 8:31-38. See also Isaiah 51:1-3 and Galatians Ch. 3
[236] See Deuteronomy 32:21
[237] Romans 1:16

238 See Romans 11:32
239 See Romans 11:24
240 See Deuteronomy Chapter 28
241 See Matthew 15:24 and Luke 19:9-10
242 See Zechariah 14:2-5, Matthew 23:39 and Acts 1:11
243 1 Corinthians 1:22
244 See Leviticus 17:10-14
245 See Judges 1:21
246 See John 10:10
247 See Genesis 1:27-28
248 See Genesis 3:17-19 and Romans 5:12-21
249 See Ephesians 6:10-20 and 2 Corinthians 10:3-5
250 See Acts 9:19-20
251 Hebrews 11:6
252 See Ephesians 4:14-15
253 See 2 Timothy 2:4-16
254 See Ephesians 6:15
255 See Matthew 5:17-18 and Luke 4:16-21
256 See Ephesians 6:18, 1 Thessalonians 5:17 and Luke 11:5-10 &18:1
257 See 2 Timothy 2:15 and 3:14-17
258 See Matthew 28:19-20 and 1 Thessalonians 2:8-13
259 See Philippians 2:12-13
260 See Romans 12:1-2, Ephesians 5:13-17 and 1 John 5:14-15
261 John 15:10-13
262 1 John 4:20b
263 See James 2:14-18
264 1 Corinthians 12:14-15
265 1 Corinthians 12:18
266 1 Corinthians 12:27
267 See 1 Corinthians 13:12
268 See Ephesians 4:13
269 See 1 Corinthians 12:7-13 and Romans 12:4-8
270 See Ephesians 4:7-16
271 See Ephesians 2:11-22, 1 Peter 2:4-10 and Isaiah 56:3-8
272 See Ephesians 4:11-16
273 See Eph. 4:15
274 See Acts 11:29-30, 2 Corinthians 8 & 9
275 See Acts 11:27 and 1 Thessalonians 6-10
276 See Matthew 24:45-51 and 25:14-30
277 See Ephesians 4:7 and 1 Corinthians 12:7
278 See Romans 12:3-8
279 See Acts 1:9-11, Matthew 24:30-31 & 24:38-41 and Luke 17:30-34
280 See James 2:17
281 See John 10:1-18

[282] See 1 Corinthians 3:1-2
[283] 2 Timothy 2:15
[284] See 1 Corinthians 1:18-2:16
[285] See John 1:1-2 and Revelation 19:11-16 especially verse 13
[286] See 1 Corinthians 3:10-15
[287] See Ecclesiastes 7:16-18
[288] See the beginning of each of his letters to the congregations
[289] See Psalms 138 especially verse 1 in the NIV
[290] See Acts 1:8
[291] See Acts 11:27-30, Romans 15:25-27 and 2 Corinthians ch. 8 & 9
[292] See Acts 15:1-2 & 21:17-19
[293] See John 10:10
[294] James 1:17a
[295] See Acts 9:30
[296] See Galatians 2:7-9
[297] 2 Corinthians 6:14 (NIV)
[298] See Matthew chapter 25
[299] Revelation 3:15-16
[300] It Works: How and Why. Narcotics Anonymous World Services, Inc., Chatsworth California, 1993.
[301] The call to discipleship is an invitation to accept and follow Yeshua. See also Matthew 4:18-22 & 28:18-20 and Mark 1:14-20.
[302] As it reads in the New International Version
[303] As it reads in the King James Version
[304] 1 Corinthians 10:13
[305] See John 12:31 & 17:14-18
[306] See also Romans 1:21-32
[307] See Matthew 12:25-30
[308] See Romans 1:18-32
[309] Isaiah 54:17
[310] Acts 26:6-7
[311] Acts 26:9
[312] John 14:6
[313] See 1 Corinthians 1:20-31
[314] See Matthew 6:24, 2 Corinthians 6:14-7:1, 1 John 1:5-6 & 2:3-6 &3:5-6, and Revelation 3:15-16
[315] Matthew 7:19-23
[316] See 1 Timothy 1:13
[317] See 1 Peter 4:14-16 (but read the whole chapter when you get a chance)
[318] See Acts 9:26-28
[319] See 1 John 1:5-7
[320] See Matthew 28:18-19
[321] See Romans 11:13-21
[322] See Hebrews 3:1
[323] See Malachi 4:5-6

[324] See Matthew 11:12
[325] See John 14:12-14
[326] See 2 Corinthians 5:21
[327] See also Isaiah 61:10, Zechariah 3:3-5 and Revelation 3:4-5 & 19:7-8
[328] Psalm 1:5
[329] See Mark 8:38
[330] See Hebrews 4:1-11

www.ingramcontent.com/pod-product-compliance
Lightning Source LLC
Chambersburg PA
CBHW052030070526
44584CB00016B/1977